Irish politics today

MANCHESTER
UNIVERSITY PRESS

Politics Today
series editor: Bill Jones

Irish politics today

Fourth edition

Neil Collins and Terry Cradden

Manchester University Press
Manchester and New York

distributed exclusively in the USA by Palgrave

Copyright © Neil Collins and Terry Cradden 1989, 1991, 1997, 2001

The right of Neil Collins and Terry Cradden to be identified as the authors of this work has been asserted by them in accordance with the Copyright, Designs and Patents Act 1988.

First edition published 1989 by Manchester University Press
Second edition published 1991 (reprinted 1993)
Third edition published 1997

This edition published 2001 by
Manchester University Press
Oxford Road, Manchester M13 9NR, UK
and Room 400, 175 Fifth Avenue, New York, NY 10010, USA
http://www.manchesteruniversitypress.co.uk

Distributed exclusively in the USA by
Palgrave, 175 Fifth Avenue, New York,
NY 10010, USA

Distributed exclusively in Canada by
UBC Press, University of British Columbia, 2029 West Mall,
Vancouver, BC, Canada V6T 1Z2

British Library Cataloguing-in-Publication Data
A catalogue record for this book is available from the British Library

Library of Congress Cataloging-in-Publication Data applied for

ISBN 0 7190 6173 3 *hardback*
0 7190 6174 1 *paperback*

This edition first published 2001

10 09 08 07 06 05 04 03 02 01   10 9 8 7 6 5 4 3 2 1

Typeset
by Ralph J. Footring, Derby
Printed in Great Britain
by Biddles Ltd, Guildford and King's Lynn

Contents

Tables

Preface

This fourth edition is marked by two major changes as compared with its predecessors. First, a full chapter – written with Mary O'Shea – is devoted to the 'new' phenomenon of corruption in the politics of the Irish Republic. This places consideration of corruption within a clear historical and analytical framework – one that we hope provides insight into the reasons for corruption, facilitates international comparison and provides a basis for some remedial recommendations. Second, we make no apology for having expanded the coverage of Northern Ireland quite considerably. A goodly portion of this is justified by the need to spell out the content and institutional effects of the Belfast 'Good Friday' Agreement. However, we have also tracked in some detail, for the period April 1998 to February/March 2001, the difficulties experienced in implementing the Agreement. The important purpose of this is to offer readers some understanding of the political and diplomatic complexities involved in reconciling the (almost) irreconcilable.

Notwithstanding these changes, a central message of this book remains the same as it was in all three previous editions: in face of claims that the politics of the Republic of Ireland defy 'standard' analyses, we persist in believing that they *can* be understood by application of the theories and concepts that political scientists would apply elsewhere – the politics of Ireland clearly do follow patterns similar to those found in other small states. The main difficulty with what we have previously described as the *sui generis* approach is that one gets little idea about whose interests routinely prevail in Irish politics. Something strongly reinforced by our consideration of corruption is the need to ask questions about the distribution of resources – taxes, grants, subsidies, rebates, permissions, restrictions and so on. Who wins or loses in these cases? And why? Does policy ignore some people, and favour others disproportionately? So as well as describing the institutions and mechanisms of politics in Ireland, we have continued to try to discern the 'patterns of power'.

We remain grateful to Frank McCann, co-author of the first two editions, whose stamp is still apparent. We are indebted too to numerous public servants, colleagues and students for their help in the updating of this book. Now the length of Ireland apart, as opposed to just a flight of stairs when the third edition was being written, we ought perhaps to give thanks for the magical facility of e-mail – but who do we thank for that? It is easier to identify the people to whom we owe most, and easier still to put our thanks in the same way as last time: Miriam and Margaret and our home-based children are due a special word of gratitude – for their much tested but enduring equanimity. Particular thanks to Lucy Cradden for help with the index.

NC, TC

Abbreviations

ATGWU	Amalgamated Transport and General Workers' Union (as the British TGWU is known in Ireland)
C&A-G	Comptroller and Auditor-General
CAP	Common Agricultural Policy
CFSP	Common Foreign and Security Policy
CIRA	'Continuity' IRA
CIU	Congress of Irish Unions
DIRT	deposit interest retention tax
DL	Democratic Left (political party)
DUP	Democratic Unionist Party
ECB	European Central Bank
EMU	Economic and Monetary Union
EPC	European Political Cooperation
EU	European Union
FWUI	Federated Workers' Union of Ireland
GNP	gross national product
IBEC	Irish Business and Employers' Confederation
ICMSA	Irish Creamery Milk Suppliers' Association
ICTU	Irish Congress of Trade Unions
IDA	Industrial Development Authority
IFA	Irish Farmers' Association
INLA	Irish National Liberation Army
IRA	Irish Republican Army
IRSP	Irish Republican Socialist Party
ITGWU	Irish Transport and General Workers' Union
ITUC	Irish Trade Union Congress
LAC	Local Appointments Commission
LVF	Loyalist Volunteer Force
MEP	Member of the European Parliament
MP	Member of Parliament

NATO	North Atlantic Treaty Organisation
NESC	National Economic and Social Council
NICS	Northern Ireland Civil Service
NIO	Northern Ireland Office
NPM	new public management
P2000	Partnership 2000
PAC	Public Accounts Committee
PCW	Programme for Competitiveness and Work
PDs	Progressive Democrats (political party)
PESP	Programme for Economic and Social Progress
PLAC	Pro-Life Amendment Campaign
PNR	Programme for National Recovery
PPF	Programme for Prosperity and Fairness
PR	proportional representation
PUP	Progressive Unionist Party
RIRA	'Real' IRA
RTÉ	Radio Telefís Éireann – the Irish state radio and TV broadcaster
RUC	Royal Ulster Constabulary
SDLP	Social Democratic and Labour Party
SEA	Single European Act
SIPTU	Services, Industrial, Professional, Technical Union
SMI	Strategic Management Initiative
SPCs	strategic policy committees
SPUC	Society for the Protection of the Unborn Child
STV	single transferable vote – a PR electoral system
TD	Teachta Dála, a Deputy or Member of the Dáil
UDA	Ulster Defence Association
UDP	Ulster Democratic Party
UFF	Ulster Freedom Fighters
UK	United Kingdom
UKUP	United Kingdom Unionist Party
UN	United Nations
UUP	Ulster Unionist Party
UVF	Ulster Volunteer Force

Words in Irish

Aer Lingus	The Irish national airline
Bord Fáilte	The Irish Tourist Board – literally, the Board of Welcomes
Bunreacht na hÉireann	The Irish Constitution
Ceann Comhairle	The Speaker of the Dáil
Cumainn	Literally 'clubs'; but used as shorthand for political party constituency associations
Cumann na nGaedheal	Early pro-Treaty governing party – usually translated as 'League of the Gaels'; merged with other groups in 1940s to form Fine Gael
Dáil Éireann	Lower house of the Irish Parliament
Fianna Fáil	Largest political party in the Republic – usually translated as the 'Soldiers of Destiny'
Fine Gael	Second largest party in the Republic – usually translated as 'Tribes of the Gael'
Foras Teanga	The North–South Language Body – a cross-border implementation agency aimed at promoting the Irish and Ulster-Scots languages
Forfás	Policy and advisory board for industrial development
Gaeltacht	Irish-speaking area
Garda	Police; the full title of the police service is An Garda Siochána, which literally translated means Guardians of the Peace
Gardaí	Police officers
Macra na Feirme	Young Farmers' Association
Oireachtas	Irish Parliament
Punt	The Irish pound, or unit of currency
Radio Telefís Éireann	Irish Radio and Television

Seanad Éireann	Upper house, or Senate, of the Irish Parliament
Sinn Féin	Name of republican political party – usually translated as 'Ourselves Alone'
Tánaiste	Deputy Prime Minister
Taoiseach	Prime Minister
Teachta Dála	Deputy or Member of the Dáil – abbreviated as TD
Teanga	Language; prefaced by the definite article 'an' – as in An Teanga – it is generally taken to mean the Irish language
Teilifís na Gaeilge	Irish-language television channel
Telecom Éireann	Former national telephone company
Udarás na Gaeltachta	The economic development body for Gaeltacht regions

1

Ireland: what kind of state?

There are many aspects of life in Ireland that Irish people, as well as visitors to Ireland, regard as special and even unique. Politics in Ireland is no exception, for the Irish at home and abroad are a very political people. The story of Ireland is reflected in a rich tradition of literature, music, myth and involvement in politics. It is easy, therefore, to concentrate on what sets Ireland apart and to fail to see it in its wider context. Indeed, many books on Irish politics present a picture so full of scheming clerics, strange parties and manipulative politicians as to leave the reader more bemused than informed. Ireland, it seems, is always different.

In this chapter, using a broad brush, we aim to put Ireland in its rightful and comprehensible place as an interesting example of a small, European, post-colonial, liberal democratic, capitalist state, attempting to solve political problems of a kind common to other such countries, but in the light of its own particular conditions.

Some historical background

The island of Ireland contains two jurisdictions: Northern Ireland, which is part of the United Kingdom (UK); and the Republic of Ireland. The Republic, which for convenience is usually referred to as Ireland in this book, became politically independent from the UK in 1922, as the Irish Free State. It is composed of twenty-six of the thirty-two counties into which the island had been divided for local government administrative purposes prior to partition – the area designated as 'Southern Ireland' in the British Government of Ireland Act 1920.

The island of Ireland became inhabited comparatively recently. Until approximately 9,000 years ago it was apparently too cold to be attractive to humans. Since then, however, there have been invasions by several peoples – of whom the Celts were just one – and each of these incursions has had

significant cultural and/or socio-political consequences. In political and institutional terms, Britain left the greatest legacy, reinforcing its grip on Ireland
by the settling, or 'plantation', in the seventeenth century of English and
Scottish Protestants loyal to the Crown, on land confiscated from the overwhelmingly Roman Catholic native population. The Tudor state stamped its
authority firmly on the country by this means and by 1603 English rule had
superseded that of the traditional Gaelic chiefs throughout most of the island.
Despite periods of resistance, and the existence for a time of its own Parliament,
Ireland was essentially subject to rule by Britain, in one form or another, until
the years just before independence in the early 1920s.

Resistance to British rule was frequently influenced by developments abroad.
When the Americans rebelled in the 1770s, Irish parliamentarians, their case
buttressed by the existence of a military force of 'Volunteers', pressed for more
legislative autonomy for Dublin. Again, in 1789, the French Revolution encouraged the open organisation of agitation for parliamentary reform and
national unity. What was to become a tradition of resistance by military means
was reinforced in the 1798 rebellion when, with the promise of French assistance, a Protestant radical named Wolfe Tone sought the subversion of British
rule in Ireland.

However, neither parliamentary nor military methods achieved the establishment of the more independent Irish political institutions being demanded.
Indeed, the opposite was the case, for the existing Irish Parliament, limited
though its powers were, was soon to be abolished. Nor did these efforts achieve
a greater unity of purpose between Catholics and Protestants, which was
another ambition of the leadership of both forms of action. The '98 rebellion
actually served to underline the separateness of the two religious groups, for
the bulk of the native Irish population remained devoted to Catholicism and
was alienated from what was in effect the British Protestant state in Ireland.

The Great Famine

The population of Ireland had almost doubled between 1800 and 1844, to
nearly 8.5 million. But one-third of Irish people were living at or below subsistence level, depending for work on an inefficient system of farming and for
their diet almost exclusively on the potato. Industry flourished only in the
north-east of Ireland, where there was a Protestant settler majority; in
contrast, Britain's industrial revolution had made it the world's manufacturing giant.

The Great Famine thus exacerbated an already unhappy situation. The
Famine resulted from the failure of the potato crop in successive years, and
the crisis lasted from 1845 to 1851. More than 1 million people died of star-
vation and 1.5 million people emigrated, mainly to Britain and the USA. (It is
worthy of note that between 1847 and 1911 the Irish population fell by well

over 40 per cent, to 4.4 million.) The Famine also had a major impact on Irish social structures, patterns of landholding and commerce. It created as well a large and embittered American diaspora of Irish rural origin, for whom the British were the guilty party in not providing sufficient food and other economic aid to prevent the tragedy.

The politics of the union with Great Britain

The Act of Union of 1801 had been intended to bind Ireland more closely to Britain; so while many state functions continued to be administered in Dublin, from then on Ireland was governed from London, with a senior Cabinet minister as Irish Chief Secretary. Irish constituencies returned Members of Parliament (MPs) to Westminster on a franchise similar to that in England. Throughout the nineteenth century, modern democratic institutions such as disciplined parliamentary groupings and mass party organisation also developed in Ireland, principally during the periods of political leadership of Daniel O'Connell and Charles Stewart Parnell. In the early part of the century, O'Connell focused on the repeal of the 'Penal Laws', which forced Catholics into an inferior social, political and economic position. Later Parnell took up the issues of land reform and Home Rule. Both set new standards in political oratory and in astute parliamentary manoeuvring. Although neither achieved all of his objectives, they together laid the foundations of popular respect in Ireland for parliamentary democracy. Their legacy survives in the primary place given to parliamentary institutions and to parliamentary methods by Irish political leaders down to the present day.

By the end of the nineteenth century also, a system of local government and a public service based on the new British principle of recruitment on merit – rather than by social rank or influence – were well established in Ireland. By the first decade of the twentieth century, the Irish were thus enjoying the same or similar levels of welfare, educational and property rights as other UK subjects. Only in the most senior public positions was the Anglo-Irish Protestant elite still firmly entrenched.

Home Rule or independence?

By the 1890s, popular sentiment for what was called 'Home Rule' was being expressed mainly through the Irish Parliamentary Party, which held the great majority of the parliamentary seats in Ireland. Home Rule was shorthand for the restoration to Ireland of a parliament subordinate in certain respects to the British government but with general autonomy over domestic legislation. From 1870 onwards it became the main rallying call for those Irish hostile to British rule. Two Home Rule Bills, intended to give Ireland limited self-government within the Empire, were defeated in the UK Parliament in the late nineteenth century.

By using its numerical strength and the pivotal voting role that this gave it in a British Parliament split between Conservatives and Liberals, the Irish Parliamentary Party managed, at the third attempt, to secure the Home Rule Act of September 1914. But it was never to take effect; the Great War (now usually called the First World War) had begun in August and the implementation of the Act was postponed for the duration of hostilities. Partly as a consequence, the initiative in the campaign for some form of independence passed from the parliamentarians to revolutionary militants.

1916 – the Easter Rising and its aftermath

The Easter Rising of April 1916 marked the beginning of the military campaign for independence. This Rising against the British presence in Ireland was an initial failure, involving about 2,000 insurrectionists, mainly in Dublin. A few hundred people were killed and much damage done in Dublin city centre. Public reaction, as far as can be judged by contemporary Dublin newspapers, was initially hostile. However, the public began to favour the militants following the execution of their leaders and the jailing of many others. At the 1918 general election, militant candidates running under the Sinn Féin banner routed the more moderate Irish Parliamentary Party. Though now subject to more critical historical analysis, the 1916 Easter Rising has a major symbolic importance in Ireland. The 'heroic failure' is still seen by many nationalists as the 'blood sacrifice' that was necessary to awaken the Irish to a sense of their nationhood.

Remarkably, therefore, it was the failure of their armed revolt that gave the much less prevalent militaristic or 'republican' tradition of Irish nationalism the political upper hand. The execution by the British authorities of the leaders of the Easter Rising in 1916 had several effects:

- it produced an angry public mood at what was seen to be a disproportionately punitive response;
- it gave retrospective justification for the resort to arms;
- and it provided a legitimation for later episodes of 'armed struggle'.

Thus when the Great War ended Britain found itself dealing with much more radical politicians. Sinn Féin rejected Home Rule, demanded total independence from Britain and won an overwhelming majority of Irish seats at the 1918 UK general election.

Rather than present themselves to take their places at Westminster, in 1919 the Sinn Féin MPs formed their own Parliament in Dublin, Dáil Éireann, which effectively became the political arm of the militant independence movement. The British sought for long, but unsuccessfully, to suppress it by force of arms. However, by 1921 both parties were weary of the struggle. As a result, among other things, the partition of Ireland prescribed in the Government of Ireland Act 1920 – which had set up Northern Ireland as a mini-state within the United Kingdom (see Chapter 7) – was essentially confirmed in the negotiations that culminated in the Anglo-Irish Treaty of 1921. The Treaty also had a decisive effect on the development of politics in independent Ireland: Sinn Féin split over the Treaty and a bitter civil war between the opposing factions followed. The roots of what are still the two main political parties in Ireland can be traced to this: Fianna Fáil emerged from the anti-Treaty tradition, while Fine Gael has a pro-Treaty lineage.

Bunreacht na hÉireann – the Irish Constitution

The political institutions of Ireland, which will be examined in greater detail in subsequent chapters, are – for the most part – based on the Westminster model. Indeed, because of the wide range of functions devolved from London to the Chief Secretary's Office in Dublin Castle, the Irish Free State inherited an almost complete administrative apparatus, together with other important state agencies, at its formation in 1922. It thus had little difficulty in grafting on new ones to cope with tasks, like defence and foreign affairs, which had formerly been reserved completely to London. So compared with many other newly independent states, at this institutional level in particular, Ireland enjoyed a fairly smooth transition.

The Constitution of the Free State was replaced in 1937, although there was considerable continuity with the previous one. The architect of the new Constitution, Bunreacht na hÉireann, was the then Taoiseach (Prime Minister), Eamon de Valera, the leader of Fianna Fáil and former chief of the anti-Treaty forces in the Civil War. This is the Constitution that remains in force today. Although it will be discussed in much greater detail in Chapter 5, it is useful at this point to outline its main features, which include:

- *the republican nature of the state* – an elected but non-executive President is head of state (although the Republic was not formally declared until 1948);
- *the unitary nature of the state* – the Oireachtas (state Parliament) is the supreme law-making body, though it must not enact laws repugnant to the Constitution and has, since 1973, had to take account also of obligations to the European Union (EU) (see below);
- *the separation of powers* – the organs of government are divided into executive, legislative and judicial, each with limited and distinct functions;
- *a bicameral (two-chamber) legislature* – the Oireachtas is composed of an upper house, Seanad Éireann (the Senate), and a lower house, Dáil Éireann, together with the President;
- *a government* – to carry out executive functions within the constraints of the Constitution and the law;

• *independent courts* – which incorporate the judicial power; the court of final appeal is called the Supreme Court.

Each of the institutions referred to in the Constitution – the presidency, the Oireachtas, the government and the courts – is given specific powers, to be exercised in accordance with the general principles of a British-style parliamentary democracy. However, the Constitution does have some significant non-British features: the fact that the Constitution is written, and that it contains provision for US-style judicial review, means that governments and legislators must take particular care to act within its requirements and stipulations. Some of these, though, are very general and thus quite difficult to interpret. For example, many of them reflect the social thinking of the mid-1930s, especially that of the Catholic Church. (Article 44, deleted in 1974, actually recognised the 'special position' of the Roman Catholic Church – as the church to which the majority of the state's citizens belonged.) Furthermore, some important conventions are not stated explicitly; for example, as in the United States, political parties are not formally recognised. The courts are, in any case, the final arbiters of what is or is not constitutional; and the only method of altering the Constitution is by a referendum of the people.

Given the changing social structure of Ireland, it seems likely that aspects of the Constitution and the system of law associated with it will change at an accelerating rate over the next few years. The Constitution specifically allows for continuity of previous statutes and the British common law tradition – provided these are not inconsistent with its own provisions. Such inconsistencies have occasionally arisen and there was formerly a tendency for Irish legislators and judges to look to Britain for ideas on statute and precedent. Recently, however, there has been a greater willingness to be innovative, especially on the part of the judiciary. Irish politics today are thus becoming less 'British' in their texture, as politicians, bureaucrats and jurists reflect the experience of eighty years of self-government and of a great deal more contact with the wider world.

A particular boost to this process of change, especially in economic terms, has been provided by Ireland's membership of the EU and its predecessor bodies.[1] As will be outlined in later chapters, the EU and its governing treaties introduced an important new source of policies, laws and court rulings into Irish politics. Beyond institutional influences, Ireland has also increased its openness to change through a deliberate expansion of its trading relations, mainly with Europe but also with the rest of the world.

An Teanga – the Irish language

In many regions of world the language of the 'metropolis', or of the colonising power, has displaced an ancient local language. So it is in Ireland. But despite the overwhelming predominance of English, Irish is constitutionally the 'first national language' and Bunreacht na hÉireann recognises English merely as the second official language. Seeking to acknowledge that English is in fact the first language of the great majority of Irish citizens, in 1996 the Constitution Review Group (see Chapter 5) called for English to be recognised as of equal status to Irish.

Some limited measure of the extent to which Irish is now being spoken can be gained from the 1991 census. There are ostensibly more than 1 million Irish-speakers in the Republic, but this figure, representing 31.6 per cent of the population, is in truth an overestimate of the numbers who can speak the language competently and actually use it regularly. Regrettably, in cultural terms, Irish is now spoken as a first language for the most part only in areas known as the Gaeltacht, situated mainly along the western seaboard.

How did this come about? During early British rule, as well as seeking to put down the Catholic religion, the authorities also sought to suppress the use by the native, Gaelic, people of their own tongue. There was also a conscious Anglicisation of manners and dress as well as language by the Irish gentry in the eighteenth and nineteenth centuries – though this was mainly for economic and commercial rather than social reasons. However, 'the lower classes of the Gaelic population' were more resistant to change: 'in the face of all discouragements they clung to the Irish language, which remained until the nineteenth century the strongest bulwark of the native tradition'.[2]

Driven as much by political as by cultural considerations, there was a growth of a more general interest in the Irish language (and in other aspects of traditional culture) in the late nineteenth century, known as the 'Gaelic Revival'.[3] Despite numerous setbacks, the influence of the Revival has endured sufficiently to affect the educational and social policies of Irish governments down to the present day. Yet official efforts to have Irish more widely used have generally failed – perhaps because most of them were marked by an element of compulsion. As well as Irish being a core school subject at both primary and secondary levels, fluency in Irish was for long a prerequisite not just for acceptance into a teaching post, but also for almost all other appointments in the civil and public services, and for admission to university.

Because of the evident failures of compulsion, there has been a policy shift in the last twenty years or so towards what might be described as exhortation and facilitation. To give just a few examples: there is enhanced government funding for industrial development in the Gaeltacht; several national agencies exist to encourage and preserve the use of the language; and there are nationally available Irish-language radio and television channels. Some government assistance is also being given to the setting up of Irish-speaking schools outside the Gaeltacht, in response – portentously perhaps – to parental demand in urban areas. This reminds us that the language remains an important part of national culture and many non-Irish-speakers support attempts to safeguard its place in education, broadcasting and official business.

The Irish economy before independence

Although until the Act of Union Ireland's own Parliament had at least some powers over trade and trading relationships, the Irish economy was managed largely in the interests of Britain – which was of course in the process of becoming the world's most powerful capitalist country. Under the Union, with a single Parliament at Westminster, the two islands became, for most purposes, a free trade area. Although several Irish industries – leather, silk, glass, hardware, furniture and wool – were permitted to retain the protection of an import tariff for a time, by 1824 all duties between Ireland and Britain had been abolished. An economically weak Ireland was thus tied to open trading with an area experiencing huge economic growth; this put it at a great disadvantage compared with most of the rest of the UK.

It remained economically underdeveloped for the greater part of the nineteenth century, therefore, with the majority of its population dependent on a subsistence agriculture. Ireland was, as the Great Famine demonstrated (see above), extremely vulnerable to the vagaries of nature as well as to the laws of the market. At the beginning of the twentieth century, the main characteristic of the Irish economy remained its dependence on agriculture and, more particularly, on the export of live cattle to Britain. By the outbreak of the Great War Ireland enjoyed an almost monopoly position in supplying the British market with agricultural produce.

Developing the economy of independent Ireland

It lay at the core of the case of the advocates of Irish independence that economic underdevelopment and the resulting poverty and emigration were the outcomes of deliberate government policy. Deprived of the more prosperous and industrialised north-east of the country as a consequence of the Government of Ireland Act, therefore, one of the greatest challenges facing the Free State was to improve the performance of its economy.

The first problem to be tackled was that agricultural exports had declined sharply after the Great War, in the face of increased competition from Denmark, New Zealand and elsewhere. The new government took immediate action to help recover export markets, especially those in Britain, and the short-term results were impressive. The export of dairy produce increased dramatically, as did the overall value of agricultural exports. However, world events militated against the maintenance of the improvement.

As a key international player, Britain underwent a severe economic crisis in the late 1920s following the collapse of global financial markets. The UK government reacted by erecting barriers against foreign goods coming into Britain and by the early 1930s a general tariff on all imports had been introduced. Access to the UK market was also restricted by other government measures affecting food products – introduced in the interests of its own farmers. Ireland was obviously affected by the general world recession also and although the governing party, Cumann na nGaedheal (the predecessor of Fine Gael), was generally in favour of free trade, it too imposed tariffs on food imports.

Protectionism

A change of government in 1932 brought a more determined move away from free trade and towards protectionism. This reorientation had a political as well as an economic basis. De Valera, the leader of the new government party, Fianna Fáil, had a particular vision of Ireland, expressed most clearly in a famous radio broadcast made on St Patrick's Day in 1943:

> That Ireland, which we dreamed of, would be the home of a people who valued material wealth as the basis of right living, of a people who were satisfied with frugal comfort and devoted their leisure to the things of the spirit – a land whose countryside would be bright with cosy homesteads, whose fields and villages would be joyous with the sound of industry, with the romping of sturdy children, the contest of athletic youths and the laughter of comely maidens, whose firesides would be forums for the wisdom of serene old age. It would, in a word, be the home of a people living the life that God desires that man should live.[4]

Plainly in keeping with this vision, Fianna Fáil had developed a policy of economic self-sufficiency. This was to be achieved by protecting the home market with tariffs on imports, thereby giving existing domestic producers a better chance of surviving and providing incentives to encourage the establishment of new indigenous industrial enterprises. Under the previous government, a producer had had to argue a case *for* protection; significantly, under the new dispensation, protection was to be given unless a case could be made *against* it. Giving effect to this, the 1932 Emergency Imposition of Duties Act gave the government wide powers to impose, vary or revoke customs duties as and when it wished. Within a few months, Ireland became one of the most heavily protected markets in the world; by 1937, imports of some 1,947 different items were controlled by this means.

Nevertheless, the late 1930s brought renewed difficulties for Irish farmers, all the more so as the government tried to diversify production behind trade barriers. A system of guaranteed prices with restrictions on imports brought an emphasis on food crops for home consumption, but decline had set in. To add to these problems there was a short but acrimonious dispute known as 'the economic war', sparked by the Irish government's refusal to pass on land annuities (essentially mortgage payments) owed to Britain by farmers who had bought property using government loans under the Land Acts of the nineteenth century. Fianna Fáil's case was that these payments were imperialistic and demeaning to Ireland and its people. Britain responded by increasing tariffs on its imports from Ireland; the Irish, in turn, erected similar barriers against British goods entering Ireland.

The row finally ended in 1938 with a general agreement on reducing tariffs between the two countries and – a curious concession given the rumbling intimations of trouble to come from Hitler's Germany – the handing into Irish control of the naval facilities (or 'Treaty Ports') which Britain had retained in Ireland under the 1921 Treaty.

The Second World War

The new Irish state had been largely preoccupied by affairs within its own boundaries during the early years of its existence. But the ending of partition – by drawing Northern Ireland into a united Ireland of thirty-two counties – remained on the agenda of all political parties in the state. Fianna Fáil took a particularly strident anti-partition view and de Valera insisted that neutrality in the Second World War was his government's only possible option for so long as Ireland remained divided. Although formally neutral, however, and publicly vilified by British politicians for this stance, Ireland clearly 'leaned' towards the Anglo-American Alliance. Exports to the UK continued throughout the war and much evidence has accumulated of covert activities in Ireland of benefit only to the Allied side.[5]

Access to food imports was clearly restricted during the course of the war, so there was a substantial increase in the production of crops purely for home consumption. As a result, acres under tillage were vastly increased, while the output of livestock and livestock products obviously fell as access to export markets diminished. After the war, with financial aid under the United States' Marshall Plan, Europe set about rebuilding its shattered economies. Not unexpectedly, Ireland's main contribution to European recovery came to be in the production of food for export and the official economic planning programme for the period 1949–53 accepted this as the primary policy.

Agricultural uncertainty

Agriculture thus remained the principal economic activity in Ireland and, although it has declined quite sharply in recent years, it is still a major contributor. In the late 1990s agriculture made up around 15 per cent of merchandise exports, accounted for more than 8 per cent of gross national product (GNP) and provided approximately one-sixth of total employment. (In the EU as a whole, agriculture by then contributed 3.5 per cent to GNP and provided 7 per cent of employment.) But all this masks the huge underlying changes in Irish farming since the end of the Second World War.

Successive governments maintained Ireland's essentially protectionist fiscal regime until the early 1960s, when it seemed that Ireland would soon be a member of the EU and be obliged to open up all of its protected industry to competition. In the event, the entry of the UK and Ireland was delayed until 1973; but by then, under the Anglo-Irish Free Trade Agreement of 1966, they were already operating in an almost tariff-free environment between themselves. Before 1973, moreover, the European Common Agricultural Policy (CAP) had virtually closed EU markets to Irish cattle and beef; Ireland's membership was to change all that.

In consequence, farming enjoyed particular prosperity between 1970 and 1978, as previous over-reliance on the British market decreased. Agricultural output rose at almost 4 per cent per annum, the highest recorded rate of prolonged growth, and efficiency increased dramatically through the application of new technology and improved managerial skills. But since the late 1970s Irish agriculture has experienced fluctuating fortunes and has suffered much greater uncertainty. Moreover, the future is now largely outside the control of Irish governments: through its remaining price support mechanisms and management of the market, the CAP largely determines the conditions under which Irish farm output is produced and sold.

The CAP has been very costly to maintain, so its future is in some doubt. However, whether the CAP remains in place or not, what seems likely to continue is the process by which some Irish farms become larger, more efficient and commercially run. But many will remain small, inefficient and unable to sustain their owners without substantial government and EU help. By the turn of the century, de Valera's dream of a rural Ireland made up mainly of small family farms, worked by their owners, had been massively eroded by world market conditions.

Foreign investment, industrialisation and the 'Celtic Tiger'

The Republic of Ireland's move from protection to free trade was a result of more than just the change in world conditions. The 1950s were years of increasing economic difficulty and political uncertainty. Multi-party coalition governments, led by Fine Gael, had been no more successful in solving these problems than had Fianna Fáil, so continuing unemployment, poverty and emigration put all parties under considerable pressure to rethink their economic approach. Protectionism and self-sufficiency had been tried but, while successful in creating an industrial base where none existed before, they were plainly now failing to meet the needs of the people of Ireland. Although it had its beginnings under a coalition government, the new approach that eventually emerged has come to be particularly identified with the advent of

Seán Lemass to the leadership of Fianna Fáil. A vastly experienced minister and skilled but pragmatic political operator, he succeeded de Valera in 1959.

The essential thrust of the new policy was to open the Irish economy to foreign capital. It was also becoming clear that the industries protected by tariffs and quotas were often, in the absence of competition, inefficient and complacent – and they had patently failed to absorb the loss of employment on the land. A central aim of the new policy was to increase industrial development by encouraging multinational firms to set up in Ireland. Such foreign investment, it was hoped, would increase employment, expand the domestic market, improve the balance of payments by way of exports and create opportunities for new Irish businesses to serve some of the needs of the multinationals.

The initial achievements of the new policy certainly seemed impressive. Foreign-owned firms provided 22,000 new jobs between 1973 and 1980 alone. Progress in the 1990s, however, exceeded even this promising start. In 1987, for instance, the unemployment rate was 18 per cent and in the 1980s the number of people employed actually fell by 6 per cent. But by 2001 unemployment was below 4 per cent and the workforce had grown by fully 25 per cent in the preceding decade, with huge increases in jobs in the 'high-tech' sector in particular. Thus emerged Europe's 'Celtic Tiger', so-called to emphasise the similarity between the success of Ireland in the late 1990s and that of the 'Tiger' economies of the Far East/Pacific Rim a few years earlier.

Yet as a consequence, labour shortages, as well as immigration policies designed to overcome these, have become pressing political issues. Indeed, some commentators see dangers in a situation in which nearly 50 per cent of the working population are employed in foreign firms, mostly from the United States. Nevertheless, indigenous industry has also grown substantially. Many Irish firms prosper as suppliers to multinationals and others through export-led expansion, with the United States as the largest single trading partner. Ireland has become one of the main locations for foreign direct investment by US corporations.

Among the attractions are low levels of company taxation, excellent national and international telecommunications and the availability of a highly educated workforce. Some of the other keys to Ireland's recent economic success have been pay moderation encouraged by national agreements between employers, unions and government;[6] stable public finances; and well judged use of EU support to improve Ireland's infrastructure and to encourage locally owned industry. A well known journalist warned, however, that:

It remains the case that the growth in foreign investment in Ireland coincided with extraordinary growth in the US economy. Its continuation at these levels cannot be taken for granted, nor indeed could we supply the necessary workers if it did.[7]

Ireland may then be vulnerable to a slow-down in the US economy, something which appeared a real possibility in the early part of 2001. Indeed, given this seeming dependency, on the one hand, on the success of the almost entirely unregulated free market economy of the United States and, on the other, Ireland's very evident commitment to the EU's social market model, the economic debate is neatly encapsulated in the question: 'Where's the focus: Boston or Berlin?'

Of course, developments within the EU are of considerable and very direct economic importance: in 1999, Ireland together with a majority of the other EU states adopted a common currency, the euro, controlled by the European Central Bank (ECB) in Frankfurt. Because the UK, which remains one of Ireland's major trading partners, was not one of those joining the euro, some economists advised against Ireland's membership – at least in the short term.[8] But the need to demonstrate even more political distance from Britain than was already the case seemed to weigh more heavily than immediate economic considerations. Paradoxically, moreover, Ireland has now become an even more attractive magnet for US investment, as the only English-speaking country in 'Euro-land'. So not even the loss of traditional methods of responding to changing international trading conditions – such as having its own Central Bank set Irish interest rates – deterred ministers from taking this crucial decision.

Yet Ireland's hands are not entirely tied. At the EU biannual heads of government summit in Nice in late 2000, the Irish (together with several other smaller states, as well as the UK) successfully fought off attempts to harmonise fiscal policy across the EU. What was resisted was a French proposal to have the forms and rates of taxation 'dictated' from the EU centre and to be applicable in all member states. Regardless of this notable success, however, as will be discussed further in Chapter 8, Ireland's economic choices must now broadly be made in the context of agreed priorities within the EU.

A democratic inheritance

Having achieved its independence essentially by revolutionary means, it is surely remarkable that the Republic of Ireland should be among the most stable and enduring liberal democratic states in Europe. In essence, this is because of the values passed down by the political actors who led the Irish independence movement. One of the strongest influences on this elite was the parliamentary tradition. And when the more militant independence movement developed in the early twentieth century, even its instincts remained fundamentally parliamentarian. The parliamentary tradition was all the stronger because its roots lay in the ideals of the American and French revolutions: that power resides in the people and is exercised only on their behalf by elected representatives. It is also important to note that independence was achieved without the intervention of other major powers. This made the post-independence period in Ireland less violent than in many other countries. The final factor making for stability was the ease with which power was transferred; and one of the main reasons for this was the continuance of so many political and administrative institutions.

Unlike many other countries that became independent in the twentieth century, then, the Republic of Ireland has remained a parliamentary democracy with fair and competitive elections, alternating parties in government, an independent judiciary and unchallenged civilian control of the military. It also enjoys a vigorous and variegated free press and broadcasting services of high journalistic as well as technical standards. What is perhaps a less understandable difference between Irish politics and those in many, if not most, other European countries is the absence of a clear left–right divide. A particular puzzle is that the main democratic socialist party, also the oldest political party in Ireland, has enjoyed only intermittent success at the polls. This question is addressed in Chapter 2.

Notes

1 The European Union was initially called the European Economic Community and later simply the European Community; to avoid confusion all references hereafter will be to the 'European Union' or the 'EU'.
2 J. C. Beckett, *The Making of Modern Ireland*, London: Faber & Faber, 1969, p. 38.
3 See R. Foster, *Modern Ireland 1600–1972*, London: Allen Lane, 1988, Chapter 18, section III.
4 M. Moynihan (ed.), *Speeches and Statements of de Valera*, Dublin: Gill & Macmillan, 1980, pp. 466–9.
5 See, for example, R. Fisk, *In Time of War*, London: Paladin, 1985.
6 See T. Cradden, 'Social partnership in Ireland: against the trend', in N. Collins (ed.), *Political Issues in Ireland Today*, 2nd edition, Manchester: Manchester University Press, 1999.
7 M-A. Wren, 'Are we too reliant on multinationals?', *Irish Times*, 17 May 2000.
8 P. Neary and R. Thom, 'Punts, pounds and euros: in search of an optimum currency area', *Irish Business and Administrative Research*, Vol. 18, 1997, pp. 211–25.

Further reading

Bew, P., Hazelkorn, E. and Patterson, H., *The Dynamics of Irish Politics*, London: Lawrence & Wishart, 1989.
Brown, T., *Ireland: A Social and Cultural History 1922–1979*, Glasgow: Fontana, 1982.
Coakley, J. and Gallagher, M. (eds), *Politics in the Republic of Ireland*, Dublin: Folens, 1993.
Foster, R., *Modern Ireland 1600–1972*, London: Allen Lane, 1988.
Girvin, B., *Between Two Worlds: Politics and Economy in Independent Ireland*, Dublin: Gill & Macmillan, 1989.

Kennedy, K., Giblin, T. and McHugh, D., *The Economic Development of Ireland in the Twentieth Century*, London: Routledge, 1988.

Lee, J., *Ireland 1912–1985, Politics and Society*, Cambridge: Cambridge University Press, 1989.

2

Parties, elections and electorates

Virtually all liberal democracies have competing political parties and in most European countries these parties are based on social divisions or 'cleavages'. Within the Republic of Ireland, however, the party system reflects no obvious social divisions; Ireland is similar to the United States in that the main parties stand principally on their records rather than their position on an ideological spectrum.

Before independence there were two distinct groups on the island, differentiated by culture, religion, language and class. This division was reflected in the different attitudes of the two groups to the 'national question'. To understand the development of the present Irish party system, we must examine how the struggle for national independence became dominated largely by the Catholic, Gaelic Irish.

The Protestant ascendancy

The plantations involved the replacement of the native Irish in positions of economic and political power by people relocated from Britain. The massive changes in the ownership of land caused by the plantations have been an enduring cause of social bitterness and political dissent right up to the present day. Along with the policy of plantation, attempts were made to integrate the Irish forcibly into a more English way of life. The British government sought to suppress the Gaelic language and culture, as well as the Catholic religion. This naturally created great animosity between the Irish and those they regarded as invaders. The conflict between planters and natives was further exacerbated by the struggle for the British Crown between the Protestant forces of William of Orange and the Catholic armies of James II. William's victory at the Battle of the Boyne in 1690 assured Protestant ascendancy in Ireland.

Catholic emancipation and the rise of nationalism

The struggle for Catholic emancipation reached its peak in 1829, when the rights of Catholics to vote and to sit in the Parliament at Westminster were finally secured. Despite these political gains, however, Catholic disaffection with British rule continued. As we have already noted, their economic problems were exacerbated by integration with Britain and the Great Famine was but the most dramatic manifestation of this.

Farm ownership by Catholics became an important issue and eventual success on this score was a consequence of a period of intense agitation led by radical nationalists against the Protestant land-owning class. So although Protestants had figured prominently at all stages in the struggle for Irish independence, nationalism and Catholicism effectively became synonymous at grass-roots level. For Catholics, it became clear that Ireland must have its own Parliament with the ability to regulate its trade with Britain if it was to develop economically. However, although Irish Catholics were a very small group in the UK Parliament, Irish Protestants were very aware that Catholic members would swamp them in any future Irish Parliament.

The difference in attitudes to British rule between the Protestants, mostly concentrated in the north-east, and the great majority of the rest of the population was eventually to be expressed in the shape of new Irish political parties. The general election of 1868 was the last in Ireland to be dominated by the English party labels of Liberal and Conservative. By 1885 only two parties took seats in Ireland: the nationalist Irish Parliamentary Party, led by Parnell, with a strategy of offering support to whichever English party would help the Irish claim for its own Parliament; and the Unionists, whose sole objective was to prevent Home Rule. This remained the position until the 1918 general election.

By then, arguably as a direct consequence of the execution of the leaders of the 1916 Easter Rising by the British, Sinn Féin had shifted nationalist sympathies from Home Rule within the UK to the creation of an independent Irish republic. Sinn Féin's overwhelming victory in the election led to the setting up of Dáil Éireann. The British government proscribed the Dáil in September 1919 and arrested some of its members, but it continued to meet in secret.

The War of Independence

For the next few years a guerrilla campaign or 'War of Independence' was waged against the British in Ireland. In May 1921, general elections were called for the two Parliaments set up by the Government of Ireland Act 1920. But while some battle was done in Northern Ireland, in the south not one seat was uncontested. Sinn Féin took 124 and the remaining four, the university seats, went to independents from Trinity College Dublin. This result strengthened the resolve of the nationalists and obviously undermined Britain's position. In July 1921, the War of Independence ended with the Anglo-Irish Treaty.

The Civil War

The Treaty divided Sinn Féin. Those who accepted it believed it was the most that could be won at that time – and that it laid the basis for eventually securing an independent all-Ireland state. The Treaty was passed by the Dáil, after an acrimonious debate, by sixty-four votes to fifty-seven. A further general election was held in 1922 and the result was a clear majority for acceptance of the Treaty – the anti-Treatyites won only thirty-six out of 128 seats. Twelve days after the election civil war broke out between the opposing sides. More than 600 lives were lost and the Civil War created divided loyalties and animosities that were to last for decades. It ended in May 1923, when the anti-Treaty forces laid down their arms, but they still refused to accept the legitimacy of the government or the state. Although the division of Sinn Féin over the Treaty, and the Civil War that resulted, provided the basis for the party system in the Free State, as we shall see, the Civil War 'split' itself reflects older divisions.

The break-up of Sinn Féin

In April 1923, the pro-Treaty TDs in Dáil Éireann (TD is the abbreviation for Teachta Dála, a Deputy or Member of the Dáil) organised themselves into a new party, Cumann na nGaedheal (League of the Gaels). Membership was open to anyone who supported the Treaty and the new Constitution. Remarkably perhaps, given earlier evidence of public support for the Treaty, at the general election of August 1923 Cumann na nGaedheal won only 39 per cent of the total vote, giving it sixty-three seats. The anti-Treatyites, or Republicans – reorganised by de Valera to fight the election as Sinn Féin – won 27.4 per cent of the vote and forty-four seats. Sinn Féin's electoral programme consisted of an outright refusal to sit in the Dáil or to accept the Free State.

A hint of class division?

Before examining the birth and rise of Fianna Fáil, which was to become the major force in Irish politics for many decades, we should pause to consider the influence of social cleavage on the early party system in the Free State. The system had been dominated since the 1880s by the demand for legislative independence from Britain. Catholics, who had suffered most under British rule, supported independence. The effect of the separatist struggle was to create a Catholic cross-class alliance; but latent class divisions were to become more obvious in the divide within the nationalist camp over the Treaty. In general, those groups who had most to gain from continued links with the British Empire – the larger business owners, the merchants and 'big' farmers – supported it. The Treaty preserved trade links with Britain and served to bolster these groups' economic and political position within Ireland. They supported Cumann na nGaedheal, which, in government between 1923 and 1932, followed a policy of free trade intended to protect Ireland's markets in the UK. In 1926, 97 per cent of Irish exports went to the UK (including Northern Ireland) and 76 per cent of imports came from the UK.

Landless farmers and farm labourers, on the other hand, gave their support to the anti-Treaty side. In part, this was because they shared the long-term aim of making Ireland economically self-sufficient. Such a policy would involve maintaining price supports for agricultural products – in much the same way that the EU does today – thus guaranteeing the incomes of small producers. The second, and major, plank in the 'self-sufficiency' strategy was industrial development. This too was to be achieved by protecting the domestic market from overseas competition. Protectionism inevitably attracted the support of small business people, whose firms stood a greater chance of survival when shielded against the availability of lower-priced goods from overseas. Indeed, protectionism also won the support of industrial workers, because of the increased employment opportunities that it promised. Thus the Civil War division did have some social basis and the emergence of Fianna Fáil confirmed this very clearly.

The rise of Fianna Fáil

The anti-Treaty leader, de Valera, resigned from Sinn Féin and founded a new party, Fianna Fáil (the Soldiers of Destiny), in 1926. In the general election of June 1927, Fianna Fáil won forty-four seats, while the remnants of Sinn Féin (which followed a policy of not taking its seats in the Dáil) won only five. In contrast to Cumann na nGaedheal, the party in government, Fianna Fáil claimed most of its support from the less well off sections of Irish society and it expended much effort on building up a strong organisation based on con-stituency parties (called cumainn). Further, Fianna Fáil developed policies that seemed more attuned to Ireland's needs after the worldwide economic crisis of the late 1920s. In particular, Fianna Fáil argued for protecting the domestic market.

At the general election in 1932, Fianna Fáil increased its vote by almost 10 per cent and formed a minority government with support from the Labour Party. It made further gains in 1933, enabling it to remain in office in its own right; and there it stayed for an unbroken run until 1948. As the sole party of government for this lengthy period, it was able to consolidate and extend its basis of support. First, through its attachment to protectionism and the economic strategy of self-sufficiency, Fianna Fáil won support from the business community and from farmers (at the expense of Cumann na nGaedheal). Second, by the introduction of new welfare measures, particularly the introduction of unemployment benefit, it also won over much of the urban working class (at the expense of Labour, as we shall see). In these years, therefore, Fianna Fáil developed into a classic 'catch-all' party, drawing its support from almost all sections of Irish society.

'Labour must wait'

The Irish Labour Party is the oldest party presently operating in the Republic of Ireland, having been formed as a wing of the trade union movement during the First World War. Moreover, much of its early inspiration came from one of Europe's most impressive self-taught Marxist thinkers, James Connolly – who was executed for his part in the Easter Rising. However, Labour has enjoyed only intermittent success with the voters. De Valera was himself sure that Irish politics would eventually conform to a typically European class-based model. However, he was also convinced that this would not happen until the national question had been settled; thus his famous remark that 'Labour must wait'.

Why has Ireland been different in this important respect? In part, it was because of the homogeneity of its social structure for, to begin with at any rate, the cleavages that did exist were comparatively slight. The difference also had much to do with the timing and result of the struggle for independence, which took place when the country was industrially underdeveloped and thus possessed a relatively small industrial proletariat – the natural constituency for a party of labour. Further, the Government of Ireland Act 1920 severed the industrial heartland of the island, Belfast and the Lagan Valley, from the rest of the country. In addition, the Land Acts of the late nineteenth century, which permitted farmers to buy their farms, produced a very conservative 'landed peasantry'. Although problems remained in agriculture, farm owners would not contemplate government interference in their work practices or in the allocation of land.

In such a setting, it is hardly surprising that the Labour Party faced an uphill battle. By the early 1920s, it had become a typically European democratic socialist party – containing an equally typical crypto-Marxist left wing. It was also associated with a spirited and active trade union movement. Despite that, Deputies who were principally small-town celebrities who had built up strong personal followings dominated Labour's parliamentary representation for many years. So most of them depended for their return to the

Dáil on the votes of essentially right-wing, parochially minded electors. In the cities, where it might have expected to do well, the Labour Party was almost completely outflanked by Fianna Fáil for many years. Fianna Fáil's superior grass-roots organisation and its popular socio-economic policies brought it the support of the majority of the urban working class, which left Labour on the margins.

Other social cleavages

Cultural and linguistic difference, a social cleavage that is represented in several party systems in Europe, was of relatively slight consequence in the Irish Free State. The division of the country into two separate states had largely removed the main cultural cleavage, between the Protestant unionists and the Catholic nationalists. Further, within the Free State, English was almost universally spoken and the Irish-speaking communities of the Gaeltacht never constituted a group with a distinct political identity.

Religion, another important cause of division elsewhere in Europe, was also of little relevance. Partition left the Free State remarkably homogeneous in terms of religion, with around 90 per cent of its population Catholic. Additionally, despite earlier differences with the proponents of independence, the Catholic Church soon identified itself very closely with the new state. This removed the possibility of church–state conflict and with it the chance of a political party campaigning for secularisation. Although there is an important element of Catholic dissent in Irish political culture, anti-clericalism of the kind found in some other European countries has been of little consequence.

Farming has been a force for political division in many countries and farmers' parties did emerge in Ireland in the 1920s and 1940s. One of these, appropriately named the Farmers' Party, and formed by the Irish Farmers' Union, was for a time a relatively successful minor party. But though its support was crucial for some governments, it never made an electoral breakthrough – no more than other minor parties which have appealed to just one small section of the electorate. In Ireland, successful minor-party TDs have often ended up joining one of the two major groups.

The foundations of Fine Gael

In 1933 the National Centre Party, Cumann na nGaedheal, and the National Guard merged to form Fine Gael. The National Guard, commonly known as the 'Blueshirts', had been formed as an unofficial defence force for Cumann na nGaedheal – which felt threatened by the growing popular support for Fianna Fáil and its relatively recent connections with the anti-Treaty forces in the Civil War. The Blueshirt leader, General Eoin O'Duffy, a former Garda Commissioner (or Chief of Police), actually became the President of Fine Gael. But O'Duffy's fascist predilections became an embarrassment to the party and William Cosgrave, the former leader of Cumann na nGaedheal, replaced him. Fine Gael is sometimes still taunted by its opponents with the Blueshirt tag, but the party is now as ideologically catch-all as Fianna Fáil. Both main parties refuse to define themselves conclusively as being to the left or the right.

Coalition politics

The development of Fianna Fáil itself into a catch-all party made the formation of an alternative government exceedingly difficult and it was not until 1948 that an anti-Fianna Fáil coalition became practicable. The so-called 'inter-party' governments of 1948–51 and 1954–57 involved parties whose policies, particularly on socio-economic issues, were remarkably diverse: but dissimilar parties were inevitably driven together by the dominance of Fianna Fáil. In addition, the main reason for the challenge to Fianna Fáil's predominance in the 1950s was the fact that the economy began to experience severe difficulties. Politicians from all parties had been arguing for a change in economic strategy, but it was Fianna Fáil that conclusively decided to open the Irish economy to foreign trade, when it returned to office in 1957. Tariffs and quotas on imports would be removed and incentives would be provided to foreign firms to set up in Ireland.

The change in policy did induce economic growth. This led to reductions in both unemployment and emigration and a real increase in living standards. The new economic prosperity won Fianna Fáil considerable electoral support, enabled it to win four consecutive general elections and kept it in office for another sixteen-year period. During this second era of extended Fianna Fáil rule there were several developments in the party system. First, the 1960s saw a decrease in the number of parties. In 1961, seven different parties sat in the Dáil along with six independents; by 1969, only the three major parties had seats, along with one independent. Second, the two opposition groups, Labour and Fine Gael, had become disillusioned with the coalition strategy. Both had found the previous coalitions unsatisfactory, particularly that of 1954–57. Moreover, each of them also believed that it was on the verge of an electoral breakthrough in the early 1960s. However, the failure of either Fine Gael or Labour to make any significant headway in 1969 brought the question of coalition back on to the agenda – Fine Gael won only slight improvements in its votes and seats, while Labour actually lost ground. Both parties realised that without the other's cooperation neither could expect to be in office in the near future. Consequently, they agreed a coalition strategy for the 1973 general election.

The single transferable vote

Fighting an election as a coalition can be of great value, because of the Irish electoral system. This is proportional representation (PR) by the single transferable vote (STV), in multi-member constituencies. Each constituency returns between three and five TDs. The elector can vote for *all* the candidates, listing them in numerical order of preference. A 'quota' is worked out according to the following formula:

$$\frac{\text{Total valid poll (number of votes cast)}}{\text{Number of seats} + 1} + 1$$

When a candidate reaches the quota, he or she is deemed to be elected. It is here that 'transferability' kicks in. The surplus of the candidate's votes above the quota – those votes 'not needed' to elect him or her – is then allocated to the other candidates according to the subsequent preferences recorded on the ballot papers. Thus, if two parties have a coalition pact before an election, they can ask their supporters to give their *second* preference vote to the partner party.

The benefits of a pre-election pact were very clear after the 1973 general election. Although Fianna Fáil increased its vote slightly, it lost six seats. Fine Gael also increased its vote slightly but gained four seats, while Labour dropped by 3 per cent in the poll. Nevertheless, the coalition won five more seats than their combined total in 1969, almost entirely because of the transfer of votes between them under the STV system.

PR and 'vote management'

We might pause here to reflect that truly proportional representation under the STV system would be possible only if the Republic of Ireland was treated as one single multi-member constituency, with more than 160 Dáil seats to be filled. Only then would the number of TDs from each party reflect with real accuracy the first preference votes of the electors across the country. However, proportionality has to be balanced against practicality and, most important of all, local loyalties. It is for this reason that the country is divided into a number of geographical constituencies – made up of a mixture of towns, cities, suburbs, rural areas and so on – with which their electorates can be expected to identify.

These areas must be small enough to attract such voter identification, but be large enough to produce a result that begins to reflect in reasonably proportional terms the wishes of the electorate as regards their representation in Dáil Éireann. The compromise between constituency and proportionality has produced a virtual consensus in Ireland that constituencies should have between three and five members. What this means, however, is that in a three-seat constituency a party (including, of course, any allies with which it has a pre-election pact) could accumulate less than 50 per cent of the first preference vote yet end up with two of the three seats; similarly, in a five seater, the support of less than 60 per cent of the electorate could deliver three seats to a party and its allies.

What this requires is good 'vote management', such as the example in 1973 referred to above. In the run-up to the 1977 general election, however, 'the shoe was on the other foot', as the Fine Gael/Labour coalition partners failed to note some ominous signs. After its defeat in 1973, Fianna Fáil had overhauled its organisation and had set out to capture the 'youth vote'. This section of the population was, and remains, extremely important, because around 45 per cent of Irish people – and thus a significant part of the electorate – are under twenty-five. Fianna Fáil appealed to the voters with a combination of tax reductions and new jobs, but was also highly successful in ensuring that its voters gave second and subsequent STV preferences only to other Fianna Fáil candidates. It won eighty-four seats, an increase of sixteen over its 1973 total, while Fine Gael lost eleven and Labour three. For only the second time in the history of the state had a party won over 50 per cent of the first preference votes. STV is also argued to have some important effects on the behaviour of TDs at constituency level; these are discussed later in this chapter.

The economy strikes back

Given the impressive position of Fianna Fáil in 1977, it might have been expected to be embarking on another long spell in office. This was not to be the case. The major reason for the decline in the party's popularity was its inability to deliver on its promises. With increased tension in Northern Ireland, Charles Haughey, who had become party leader and Taoiseach in 1979, singled out the unification of Ireland as the most important issue in the election of 1981. Fine Gael, by contrast, concentrated on the economy. It won more seats and votes than ever before. In the new Dáil, Fine Gael had sixty-five seats, Fianna Fáil seventy-eight and Labour fifteen. The coalition partners, with more seats between them than Fianna Fáil, agreed on a joint programme and formed a government. This coalition, which depended on the tacit support of some independents, lasted until February 1982.

The February 1982 election changed the government again, but only briefly. Fianna Fáil gained three seats, making a total of eighty-one, and formed a government with the support of one independent TD and the small Workers' Party. The new administration was able to stay in office only until November 1982. After swingeing cuts in social services, the Workers' Party withdrew its support and the government fell. In the general election that followed, Fianna Fáil lost six seats, Fine Gael gained seven and Labour one. This gave Fine Gael and Labour a combined overall majority and another coalition government was formed.

A 'new right'?

The failure of Fianna Fáil to regain its traditional position as the 'natural' governing party of the Republic precipitated a challenge to Charles Haughey's position as party leader. Opposition to him was based on his style of leadership, his stance on Northern Ireland and his conservative views on questions of personal morality, such as divorce.[1] There were also reservations about his attitude to the economy. He favoured increased spending to promote growth and job creation, while others in the party wanted more controls on expenditure. A challenge to Haughey by his main rival, Desmond O'Malley, failed and O'Malley and several other TDs eventually left Fianna Fáil to form the Progressive Democrats (PDs). The PDs are clearly on the political 'right' but, in Irish terms, are radical on some important social issues.

The demands of austerity

The main theme dominating the Dáil after 1982 was, once more, the state of the economy. The coalition had attempted to reduce Ireland's foreign borrowing, without success; and although it managed to cut the inflation rate dramatically, unemployment soared and with it emigration. In January 1987, Fine Gael introduced a budget involving widespread cutbacks in government expenditure. The Labour TDs were unable to support the welfare reductions involved so they resigned and provoked an election.

Fine Gael fought the general election on its austerity budget. The PDs adopted the economic strategy of the 'new right', including decreasing substantially government involvement in the economy, privatisation, reduced spending on welfare provision and large tax cuts. Fianna Fáil accepted that 90 per cent of the Fine Gael budget would have to be introduced, but it committed itself to investing in targeted areas to increase economic growth, to create jobs and maintain welfare benefits. Labour said that welfare benefits would have to be maintained and the tax net widened to increase the contribution made by farmers and the self-employed.

The outcome of the 1987 election was a minority Fianna Fáil government. An examination of the results, however, revealed some cause for concern for Ireland's dominant party. While Fianna Fáil voters transferred their preferences overwhelmingly to candidates within the party, these candidates received relatively few transfers from 'outside'. Further, the PDs made some significant inroads into Fianna Fáil territory, especially where former Fianna

Fáil members stood as PD candidates. Perhaps most significant for the future of the Irish party system was the growing trend for Fianna Fáil to lose support among the middle classes. Overall, Fianna Fáil received its lowest share of the vote in twenty-six years, Fine Gael its lowest for thirty years and Labour's showing was the worst for fifty-four years. In contrast, the PDs made the most dramatic debut for a new party in forty years.

The task of the minority government was eased considerably by the decision of Fine Gael to offer conditional support for its central policies. The main parties were all agreed on the need for sharp reductions in public spending and reduced government borrowing. Though it was defeated five times in the Dáil, the government lost no crucial vote. Nevertheless, the Taoiseach, Haughey, was tempted into calling an election in June 1989 – mainly, it would seem, because opinion polls were indicating that the government might win an overall majority. In the event, Fianna Fáil lost seats, despite securing 44 per cent of first preference votes – the same as in 1987. Its performance only served to emphasise Fianna Fáil's new dependence on other parties.

Fine Gael and the PDs had themselves entered into a coalition agreement during the election campaign. The PDs lost heavily, however, and although Fine Gael did improve by four seats, the parties' combined total of sixty-one was well short of the eighty-four needed for a Dáil majority. The left-wing grouping, Labour and the Workers' Party, had fared better, but ruled out any participation in government. Ireland was thus faced with several weeks of uncertainty before an apparently unlikely coalition government involving Fianna Fáil and the PDs was formed in mid-July 1989.

Whither Fianna Fáil?

The principal question for Irish politics posed by the 1989 general election was again about the future role of Fianna Fáil. Since its foundation in 1926, the party had provided single-party government on fourteen out of nineteen possible occasions. Fianna Fáil traditionally eschewed coalitions, representing itself as *the* national party; but it has failed to maintain its early hegemony.

The party's dominance of Irish politics received a further blow in November 1990, when the left-wing independent, Mary Robinson, won the presidential election. A one-time member of Seanad Éireann, and closely associated with several liberal causes, she had a comfortable victory, after the second count, over Fianna Fáil's Brian Lenihan and Fine Gael's Austin Currie. Robinson was proposed as a candidate by the Labour Party, of which she had formerly been a member, and had the support of the Workers' Party and other left-wing groupings. The PDs did not formally recommend any candidate, but several prominent members spoke glowingly of Robinson. During her campaign she rejected the description 'socialist', though her opponents referred frequently to her past support for socialism. Nonetheless, for the left in Irish politics,

Robinson's poll was taken as a sign that an attractively and sensitively presented campaign could bring electoral success.

In Fine Gael, the reverberations of their defeat were felt almost immediately. Alan Dukes, facing the prospect of a vote of no confidence from the Fine Gael parliamentary party, resigned as leader and was replaced by John Bruton. Though Fianna Fáil's share of the vote in the presidential election was the same as in the previous general election, the 1990 result represented a major disappointment. Furthermore, the presidential election was the sixth occasion under Charles Haughey at which the party had failed to win a national contest. Many Fianna Fáil supporters began to question the leadership's approach: to coalition with the PDs; to party organisation; and to the presidential campaign.

Disappointment at the presidential election was followed for Fianna Fáil by major reverses at the local government contests in June 1991. Haughey's position as leader was undermined by tension between himself and O'Malley, PD leader and coalition partner, and by unrest within Fianna Fáil itself. Having survived several direct and indirect challenges to his position, Haughey resigned from office in January 1992 when the PDs threatened to leave the coalition. Albert Reynolds succeeded Haughey as leader and the partnership with the PDs survived until November. Despite all the portents, however, many in Fianna Fáil still thought a single-party government was achievable. If the party broadened its appeal by adopting aspects of what has come to be known as 'the liberal agenda', while highlighting the instability of coalition arrangements, Fianna Fáil could, it was felt, still secure a Dáil majority. But this outlook was further shaken by the 1992 general election.

The 1992 result produced the worst vote for the party since 1927, the year it entered the Dáil for the first time. By contrast, Labour's representation increased from fifteen to thirty-three seats. In addition, although Fine Gael had been reduced from fifty-five to forty-five TDs, a return to a Fine Gael-led coalition seemed highly probable. The PDs had secured an additional four seats through an electoral strategy of concentrating on a few constituencies and the party seemed destined to be part of a 'rainbow coalition'. Following a lengthy period of discussion, however, a Fianna Fáil/Labour government was formed, based on an agreed programme, in January 1993.

A major watershed

For Fianna Fáil, 1992 was a watershed. The party faced a future as the leader in the electoral market, but one not sufficiently dominant to achieve office on its own. Its rural base remained strong, but the party recognised the need to halt the erosion of its working-class support in Dublin. The choice of Dubliner Bertie Ahern as party leader in 1994, and a change in the way it appeals for voting transfers at by-elections, signalled a new realism in Fianna Fáil.

After the 1992 election, Fine Gael also faced serious problems. It remained the Republic's second largest party but there were signs that it had lost its sense of purpose. Further, its candidate had finished third in the presidential election of 1990. Although Fine Gael had achieved 39 per cent of the popular vote at the start of the 1980s, the party failed to exceed 30 per cent in all subsequent general elections. With the formation of a Fianna Fáil/Labour coalition with the largest parliamentary majority ever, Fine Gael seemed restricted to an unpromising opposition role for the foreseeable future.

Meanwhile, the Fianna Fáil/Labour government was proceeding on the basis of a shared centre-left policy programme and similar approaches to Northern Ireland policy. The new government enjoyed early economic success, with high growth and low inflation. It also concluded a broad agreement with the UK government in December 1993, the so-called Downing Street Declaration, which was followed in August 1994 by a cease-fire by the Irish Republican Army (IRA) (see Chapter 7). Despite this good fortune, trust between the two party leaders broke down and the government fell. Fine Gael were handed a lifeline.

1994: new government, no election

The events precipitating the fall of the government were the publication of the Beef Tribunal Report in July (see Chapter 6) and disagreement over a judicial appointment in November 1994. An election was not necessary, however, since Fine Gael, Labour and the small left-wing party Democratic Left (DL) were able to agree on the formation of a new coalition government, led by John Bruton of Fine Gael, which took office in December 1994.

The Fine Gael/Labour/DL coalition proved more enduring than its ideological breadth might have suggested. It enjoyed significant success in economic policy, with the Labour Minister for Finance able to announce a budget surplus in the run-up to the 1997 general election. Some of the scandals that were soon to dominate Irish politics (dealt with in Chapter 6) were beginning to surface; but they were not yet threatening the government. The coalition partners thus put forward a joint campaign for re-election, claiming that the new prosperity would be undermined by an unstable Fianna Fáil/PD coalition. But while Fine Gael increased its seats, Labour's support declined dramatically – and DL's vote also slipped marginally (see Table 2.1).

For Fianna Fáil, 1997 did not change its share of the vote significantly. Thus, it failed to get its overall vote above 40 per cent – seen as a critical electoral threshold for any party seeking to form a government on its own. It did, however, gain nine extra seats – in another example of effective vote management under the STV system. So despite the PDs retaining only four of their six previous seats, Fianna Fáil and the PDs were able to form a minority government with the support of a number of independents. Incidentally, Fianna Fáil also fell short of 40 per cent of the votes in the European and

Table 2.1. *Results of the 1997 Irish general election*

Party	First preference votes			Seats		
	Number	%	Change	Number	%	Change
Fianna Fáil	703,682	39.3	+0.2	77	46.4	+9
Fine Gael	499,940	28.0	+3.5	54	32.6	+9
Labour Party	186,045	10.4	−8.9	17	10.2	−16
Progressive Democrats	83,765	4.7	0	4	2.4	−2
Democratic Left	44,901	2.5	−0.3	4	2.4	−
Sinn Féin	45,614	2.6	+1.0	1	0.6	+1
Green Party	49,323	2.5	−0.3	2	1.2	+1
Workers' Party	7,808	0.4	−0.2	−	−	−
Others	167,913	9.4	+3.4	7	4.2	+2

Source: T. Nealon, *Nealon's Guide to the 28th Dáil & Seanad: Election '97*, Dublin: Gill & Macmillan, 1997.

local elections in 1999, though its vote management again safeguarded its level of representation.

Following its setback at the 1997 election, DL merged with the Labour Party. DL had failed to carve out a distinctive niche to the left of Labour and seemed to be unable to capitalise on its period in government. The negotiations on the merger were complicated by rivalries at constituency and trade union levels, but they were assisted by a belief that with a broad platform the left could find a more secure electoral base. There was also a palpable sense that this merger brought Irish democratic socialists something which had been lacking for years: political unity under the historic banner of Labour.

In contrast to DL's problems, the 1997 election did see the return of what some commentators unkindly described as a 'ragbag' of seven independents, each as a result of successfully creating a high local profile on totally different and generally very parochial issues. They were joined in 2000 by a by-election victor in Tipperary South who tapped discontent with Fianna Fáil and an unwillingness on the part of the electorate to endorse the alternative mainstream parties. Sinn Féin, with one TD, and perhaps boosted by developments in Northern Ireland (see Chapter 7), has also identified a significant support base among the urban working class in the Republic, particularly at local government level. They, like the environmentally conscious Green Party, could become established niche players.

A new pattern?

For the moment, then, Ireland looks like retaining its distinctive party system, with two large catch-all parties and a varying number of smaller groupings.

The disposition of seats in Dáil Éireann in 2001 was: Fianna Fáil, 75; Fine Gael, 53; Labour, 21; PDs, 4; others, 12.

The PDs seemed to have established themselves as a permanent force, unlike the many small parties that have come and gone very quickly. But opinion poll evidence suggests that the party's future is precarious. Sinn Féin, the Greens, or indeed a loose group of independents might just gain a greater foothold. In the long run, however, it is difficult in such a small and socially homogeneous country to oust the established parties. A range of factors militates against radical changes in the party system: the conservative economic outlook of the land-owning Irish farm family; the relative smallness of the urban proletariat; the importance of the symbols of national unity; the broad consensus on social values; and the successful corporatist approach to economic policy.

Local political competition and the effects of the STV system

Still other factors have had an important effect on the way individual politicians compete for election: the stability of the party system; the lack of serious ideological divisions between the main parties; a tradition of strict party discipline in the Oireachtas; and the way Irish electors generally remain faithful to one political party. Elections are won or lost by relatively few voters switching their support and by the success of parties in persuading their traditional supporters to cast their votes. When new parties do emerge, their success is often short-lived.

But argued to be one of the strongest influences on the 'constituency behaviour' of politicians is the STV system in multi-member constituencies. This in effect obliges politicians to compete not only against the candidates of other parties, but also against fellow party nominees. Fianna Fáil or Fine Gael may win or lose, but the main priority for each politician is that he or she is personally successful. To ensure success regardless of party fortunes, a politician must have some basis of support among the electorate beyond party allegiance. Politicians of earlier generations could often rely on being supported because of their role in the struggle for independence or their stand during the Civil War. Today no candidate can be so assured. Clearly, moreover, the parties do not allow open displays of disagreement at election time, so candidates of the same party cannot compete for support based on policy considerations. Irish politicians, therefore, emphasise their local, social and personal links with the electorate.

Personal support is generally based on the exchange of favours or – perhaps more accurately – the illusion of favours, since most Irish people continue to believe that public authorities are best approached by some intermediary or 'influential' person. The basis for this belief has been said to lie in the centuries of domination by a colonial power, but it has persisted for a remarkably long time after independence. Thus, people are not identified primarily in their formal roles as lawyers, business people, councillors, ministers and so on, but in the first place as friends, or friends of friends, or relatives of friends or people with whom there is some close contact or reciprocal basis for a favour. The use of such contacts and the 'calling in' of favours are considered legitimate by those with authority and influence, as well as by those seeking to use the same. The relatively low level in Ireland of subjective civic competence – the confidence of a citizen in coping with the state and its agencies – tends to reinforce the need for local intermediaries. This has had the effect of producing politicians who are primarily brokers rather than legislators. Much of an Irish politician's time is thus still taken up with telephoning or writing to government ministers, civil servants, local government managers and others in authority on behalf of constituents.

In multi-member constituencies, then, politicians try to gather sufficient personal support to be elected ahead of their party colleagues – in other words, to be the first to reach the STV quota. Each candidate will ask voters on the doorstep for a first preference vote for himself or herself and for subsequent preferences to be given to fellow party nominees – often in accordance with some pre-agreed order. Yet the greatest rivalries in Irish politics are often within parties, rather than between them. If there are really only, say, enough votes (based on the historical record) to elect two party members in a five-seat constituency, and there are three party candidates, the battle lines are clear.[2] Cultivating a substantial personal following is seen as sure way of guaranteeing an adequate share of first preference votes; and the way to ensure such a following seems to be to offer a better 'service' to constituents than any other potential TD, including fellow party members.

Irish and foreign commentators frequently forecast the end of this 'brokerage' system in the face of increased education, wealth, sophistication and civic competence. The system remains important nonetheless. The importance of social and local connections to politicians' careers is examined further in Chapter 3.

Conclusion

The party system in Ireland is different from most European party systems, because it is not based as much as elsewhere on social cleavages. This is principally because such cleavages were relatively weak at the formation of the system. The major issue after independence in 1922 was the Anglo-Irish Treaty. The division it produced formed the basis of the Irish party set-up as we know it today. This issue has, however, subsided since the 1930s. The success of Irish parties now depends on their economic appeal to the electorate and on the loyalty of their traditional supporters.

Alternative solutions to economic problems have long been the mainstay of Irish general election campaigns. Fianna Fáil's predominance owes much to its record of advancing the economic prosperity of the country. It did this from 1932 to 1948 with its policy of economic self-sufficiency. When this strategy reached the limits of its usefulness, the electorate began to look to other parties and to vote against the incumbent government. In the four consecutive general elections of 1948, 1951, 1954 and 1957, each government was voted *out* of office.

The Fianna Fáil government of 1957 successfully developed the new economic strategy, based on industrialisation by foreign investment. The prosperity that resulted enabled it to win a further three general elections: the election of 1973 ended Fianna Fáil's second run of sixteen years in office. It also ushered in a new period of uncertainty in Irish politics.

From the beginning of the 1970s until the early 1990s, Ireland was faced with inflation, unemployment and national debt. Once again, the electorate tended to vote *against* governments: in the seven general elections from 1969 to 1987, the government lost office each time. In 1989, though it retained its share of the vote, a Fianna Fáil government was forced into a coalition for the first time, having been denied a clear majority. In 1994, moreover, a new government was formed for the first time without the need for a general election; but it in turn was defeated, in 1997. Today, therefore, coalition governments are the norm; and every party in the Dáil is now a potential government partner. Yet the major question about the Irish party system remains unanswered: when will the division created by the Sinn Féin split over the 1921 Treaty finally give way to one reflecting more explicit class or economic divisions in Irish society?

Notes

1 Haughey's views on such matters are interesting in the light of the revelation much later – in 1999 – that he had conducted a long-standing affair with a well known newspaper gossip columnist, who was also the wife of a senior judicial figure.

2 Once again, in accordance with good vote management, a party will put up three candidates in these circumstances in order to maximise its overall first preference votes – in the knowledge that even though the 'third' candidate is not going to be elected, his or her second (and subsequent) preference votes will transfer reliably to the other two.

Further reading

Busteed, M., *Voting Behaviour in the Republic of Ireland: A Geographic Perspective*, Oxford: Clarendon Press, 1990.

Marsh, M. and Mitchell, P. (eds), *How Ireland Voted 1997*, Boulder, Colorado: Westview Press, 1999.

Sinnott, R., *Irish Voters Decide: Voting Behaviour in Elections and Referendums Since 1918*, Manchester: Manchester University Press, 1995.

3

Elites and pressure groups

Power in Ireland is exercised by a range of private and public institutions, such as large companies, banks, government departments, state-sponsored enterprises (trading and manufacturing companies owned by the state) and major pressure groups. Private wealth is concentrated in relatively few hands and control of public resources is also dominated by a small number of individuals. Such a distribution of power is typical in liberal democratic capitalist societies. In this chapter we will examine the nature of the elites as well as the influence of the main pressure groups. Adopting Parry's classic definition, we will take elites to be 'small minorities who appear to play an exceptionally influential part in political and social affairs'.[1]

Studies of countries much larger than Ireland have shown remarkable levels of concentration of power. Some social theorists – notably Weber and Durkheim – have sought to show that as societies develop, individual functions within them become more specialised. To such theorists, the cohesion of a social structure demands coordinating elites. Ironically, as more avenues for individual advancement are opened and people are freed from social traditions, so more specialised power roles are created. Some level of elite coordination appears essential for social stability, therefore, even in democracies.

In Ireland, the number of people in key positions of private and institutional power is small enough for elite members to be known and accessible to each other. Members of the Irish elites may have ascended from different professional paths, but there are often common elements in their educational and social backgrounds. Similarly, some points of convergence can be shown in political and social attitudes. In general terms, the various elites accept the economic values of capitalist development, based on profit-making. The possession of private property is seen as justified and necessary and a degree of social inequality is seen as essential to the successful operation of the economic system. The approach of the political and administrative elites to economic development – an approach which requires the encouragement and defence

of manufacturing, trading and agricultural business enterprise – coincides
with that of the economic elite.

In this chapter we will examine elites by looking at people who, by virtue
of their occupation of positions of influence and control in major institutions,
can be described as 'powerful'. It is assumed that once they are in such elite
positions, their power is felt by society, whether they act consciously to influence particular decisions or not.

The economic elite

The economic elite is taken to be individuals who own substantial amounts
of productive property or who occupy top positions in the most important
firms. It has been estimated that in Ireland 1 per cent of the population owns
around one-third of the nation's wealth and 5 per cent account for nearly
two-thirds of it. By contrast, in the mid-1990s about a third of the population
lived on incomes that were less than 60 per cent of the average. These figures
have been challenged on points of detail, but the general pattern of inequality
is plain. Recent studies also affirm that in Ireland income inequality is more
marked than in most EU countries and is close to North American levels. *The
National Development Plan 2000–2006* acknowledges the persistence of this
gap:

> The benefits of Ireland's rapid economic progress over the past few years are
> evident.... However, it is clear that not everyone has benefited proportionately
> from this new-found prosperity – indeed, the disparity between high income
> earners and the socially excluded may even have widened.[2]

Personal wealth is not in itself a measure of power unless it is associated
with institutional or other public status; some wealthy people may make no
direct impact whatever on society at large. It is not clear whether Ireland's
wealthiest citizens are also part of the managerial elite that now dominates
large corporations, banks and other financial institutions. What is clear, however, is that access to political or administrative elite positions is not notably
easier for the wealthy. As will be shown below, Irish civil servants and
members of the Oireachtas are not marked out by the same social distance
from the population they serve as in a country such as Britain.

Many of Ireland's wealthiest citizens retain their wealth as agricultural
property. But on the whole the pattern of landholding is relatively static. Only
2,500 or so of Ireland's more than a quarter of a million agricultural holdings are above 300 acres and the great majority of farms have been owned
and operated by the same family from generation to generation. The land
reforms of the late nineteenth century reduced considerably the number and
influence of large landowners. By contrast, the chief executives of the biggest

agricultural cooperatives and other related businesses have become highly influential members of the economic elite. Although many of the largest firms are foreign owned, Irish business executives have been given increased prominence in recent years also and some have become active in the public domain.

Research on the economic elite in Ireland is very sparse, however, and many everyday assertions about it are little more than speculation. Yet it is apparent that the economic elite is relatively stable and exercises some 'control' over its own membership. Obviously, the privately wealthy may retain their advantage through the working of inheritance, good accountants and a relatively favourable tax regime for wealth – as distinct from income. The inter-generational stability of social groupings in Ireland is also remarkable. In a fascinating – though rather dated – study of Dublin, Whelan and Whelan examined the composition of what they called 'the elite classes':

> Thirty-five per cent of the men currently in this higher class are themselves sons of higher professional and managerial fathers; a further 40 per cent are drawn from the other white collar classes and the petty bourgeoisie. Thus, 75 per cent of the occupants of higher professional and managerial classes are drawn from just four classes; the corresponding figure for England and Wales is 47 per cent. Similarly, only 14 per cent of higher professional and managerial respondents had working-class origins, a figure which is half the corresponding one for England and Wales.[3]

Put in another way, the chances of a person born into the highest social bracket staying in that group are 240 times greater than those of someone born in the lower classes gaining membership of it. These figures are, of course, too global to apply directly to the elites looked at here. Nevertheless, the background to our study of elites is one of high social stability.

Further, in Ireland, a person's first occupation, which is heavily influenced by educational attainment, has an extremely significant effect upon where in the economic hierarchy he or she is currently employed. In effect, not many people who start in manual and semi-skilled jobs gain professional or managerial posts later in life. One reason for this social rigidity is that participation rates in higher education are many times greater for the offspring of professionals and managers than for other social categories. In addition, some children of the economic elite attend fee-paying secondary schools that offer both educational and social advantages. In confirmation of all this, a report for the Higher Education Authority in October 2000 found that courses that provided access to the professions – medicine, law, veterinary science and dentistry – remain dominated by the children of higher professionals.[4] Students from households headed by semi-skilled or unskilled workers make up a meagre 0.49 per cent of those participating at universities or other tertiary colleges.

During the first thirty years of the twentieth century, the upper or 'ascendancy' class associated with the former British regime became socially marginalised. The social elite of the new state, by contrast, was decidedly bourgeois, dominated as it was by the mercantile and shop-keeping classes. Historically the Irish bourgeoisie was based essentially on trade. Throughout the eighteenth century, Catholics were prevented from owning land, except on relatively short leases, and were also excluded from public office. They thus directed their energies and wealth into trade – a large proportion of economic activity, especially for an island. Much of the profit earned from this business was invested abroad and in commercial rather than manufacturing ventures. A main argument for relaxing the Penal Laws, as the anti-Catholic legislation was known, was to encourage the wealth held by Catholics to be invested in the country, to increase economic activity. But although these laws were abolished towards the end of the eighteenth century, in the event the Catholic bourgeoisie put little of their money into industrial development. They had almost no experience in industrial matters, in any case; and there was greater uncertainty about industrial projects in Ireland because of British competition.

At independence, therefore, the more prosperous Irish were in trade, farming and the professions. Where they were involved in industry, this tended to be on a small scale. Social mobility for smaller farmers and traders generally required entry into the traditional professions, which were highly regarded for both the status they brought and the security they provided. For the lower middle class and for people from working-class backgrounds who aspired to social improvement, it was the large bureaucracies like the civil service, local government and public administration that provided the main channel for upward mobility.

Political elites

In a democracy, public policy ought to reflect to some degree the views of the electorate. Such views are, however imprecisely, filtered through politicians. A great deal of attention is paid, therefore, to who the politicians are and how their background may influence political outcomes. In Ireland, parliamentarians share many of the same characteristics as their counterparts in other liberal democracies: they are disproportionately male and generally older and better educated than the voters they represent. In the Dáil elected in 1997, only 12 per cent were women. The largest party, Fianna Fáil, had the lowest proportion of women TDs, although those women it did have were more likely to have retained their seats than those from other parties. The typical TD in the year 2000 was over fifty years old. Over 70 per cent were over forty, which compared with 34 per cent of the adult population (all those aged over twenty-one). By the same token, the elderly were also absent – there was no TD aged over seventy. The Dáil is also atypical in terms of education,

Table 3.1. *Socio-economic background of TDs, 1996*

Categories	TDs (%)	Population as a whole (%)
Higher professional	24	4
Lower professional	28	6
Employers/managers	17	7
Semi-skilled and non-skilled manual	–	13

Source: *Report of the Constitution Review Group*, Dublin, Government Publications Office, 1996.

with over half its members having university degrees, in contrast to 10 per cent of the rest of the population. Again, better-educated TDs tend to retain their seats more successfully.

The Constitution Review Group took a comprehensive look at the characteristics of politicians in 1996 (Table 3.1). This showed that the profile of Irish public representatives is very close to that in most other Western democracies: TDs are disproportionately drawn from the liberal professions, especially teaching and law; they are also twice as likely to have completed secondary education and over three times as likely to have a university degree as the general population. Though farmers are much in evidence in the Dáil, they are under-represented in terms of their numbers in the country as a whole. The dominance of the professional classes is even more marked at ministerial level: almost 60 per cent of ministers since 1922 have come from this group. Business people are also well represented among ministers, although it is sometimes hard to know with what size of enterprises they have links.

The professional background and educational attainment of politicians do not, of course, tell us anything about their views or policy preferences. To assume, for example, that better-off individuals are less sensitive to the plight of the poor could be very wide of the mark. What the evidence does tell us is that certain groups, such as manual workers, women and the socially disadvantaged, generally do not make it to the top as politicians.

As we saw in Chapter 2, it is important for a candidate at an Irish election to become known personally to the electorate. This process is, of course, eased if one's name is an established one. Twenty-five per cent of TDs elected in 1997 were related to former members; indeed, often they are their sons or daughters. 'Heredity', for want of a better word, thus plays an important part in elite selection. Other forms of ready identification, such as sporting repute, may also help an individual aspiring to the political elite: 15 per cent of incumbents in the 1980s were prominent in sport. The 'parachuting' of well known names onto the political battlefield has, however, yielded little success. Parachuting generally occurs when a party centrally imposes a candidate on one of its local organisations because it feels that the available runners do not have a sufficiently high public profile. Indeed, more than one party may approach potential candidates such as television personalities, sports stars and pressure group leaders. What appears to happen when there is an imposed candidate is that she or he gets very little support from local party workers.

The route to the national political elite commonly involves service in local government. Almost 80 per cent of TDs have been local councillors and a record of such service helps a candidate establish his or her name in the potential Dáil constituency. Local government experience may be particularly important for a candidate without the social advantages of professional status or educational attainment.

Local government service, local family connections and local prestige are, then, the most important qualifications for entry to the political elite. Perhaps for this reason, that elite is not notable for any great social distance from the electorate – though those from lower-status occupations are at a marked disadvantage. Moreover, the membership of the Oireachtas changes only slowly, despite the highly competitive rhetoric of elections. Once elected, a TD and, to a lesser extent, a Senator can expect a reasonably long career. According to the Constitution Review Group, 83 per cent of the members of the Dáil are full-time politicians, devoting 'none' or 'not a significant amount' of their time to other occupations. This 'career path' is reflected in the occupational history of the 57 per cent of TDs who entered the Dáil after 1987. Playing its own role in this is the Seanad (see Chapter 5). Often, membership of the Seanad is used to introduce new members to the elite; it is also used as a temporary resting place for TDs who have suffered defeat at the hands of the wider electorate.

Though they are bound to emphasise partisan differences and subtly establish their own distinctive personal images, Irish politicians of whatever party have many interests and values in common. Among these are loyalty to parliamentary democracy, to nationalism and – though to a diminishing extent – to the moral ethos of the Roman Catholic Church. In light of recent corruption scandals of various kinds, it is important also to record the remarkable contradiction that while the public do not have a particularly high level of trust in politicians, they are generally happy with their conduct of the affairs of the nation (see Chapter 6).

Public servants

The political elite, as defined above, includes all members of the Oireachtas. But this is almost certainly too broad a definition if the criteria for inclusion are to include the possession of a direct and sustained influence on policy. Most backbench TDs and Senators have almost no influence whatever in this regard. One group which does is made up of those in the senior ranks of the civil service.

After independence, the Free State bureaucracy became as central an institution in the governance of the country as its British predecessor. The enormous importance of the civil service, and to a lesser extent the bureaucracies associated with state-sponsored bodies, was heightened by the dominance of the public sector in the rather underdeveloped economy of the post-independence period. It is arguably because of its political indispensability that the civil service was able to maintain a corporate integrity and identity and to resist pressures towards politicisation. The result of this situation was the survival of a powerful bureaucracy independent of the various party machines.

Here we will look primarily at the higher civil servants, those at Principal Officer level and above. In 2000, 542 people were in such positions. These posts are recognised as crucial because their occupants control vital information flows, as well as being the main sources of advice to senior political office holders. As we will see in Chapter 4, higher civil servants often make important policy decisions independently of politicians and they certainly shape policy significantly. Of course, senior politicians do get advice from outside sources, but in Ireland, more than in most democracies, power is highly centralised in the state bureaucracy.

The recruitment and promotion procedures of the Irish public service, local and national, are formally and rigorously meritocratic. Despite some occasional rumblings about favouritism in promotions, the central tenet remains the merit principle. This means that persons selected for posts in the public service must have the requisite skill and knowledge to do the job in question. Though public service recruitment is controversial elsewhere, particularly in newly independent states, in Ireland there has been no sustained challenge to the system, based as it is on the possession of qualifications. It is assumed that such an arrangement removes the dangers of inefficiency and favouritism associated with political appointments. Civil servants and local government officers are recruited by the Civil Service and the Local Appointments Commissions respectively. The political neutrality and absolute independence of these bodies are not in doubt.

Traditionally, most civil servants (other than those in specialised technical grades) joined at junior levels straight from school, but the proportion of graduate entrants has increased significantly in recent years. A similar trend towards graduate entry may occur at local government level, now that some middle-ranking posts have been opened to graduates. The traditional model for high-level public servants has been junior entry followed by in-service training, university education through evening classes and day release and a steady progress up the ranks via examinations and competitive interviews. The Departments of Finance and Foreign Affairs are exceptions in that most of their senior people enter the service as graduates.

Higher civil servants have their critics, but few can doubt their qualities of industry and dedication. Indeed, most criticisms have centred on the presumed dulling effects of such sustained practical and diligent work in a hierarchical organisation. The civil service is accused of being too unimaginative, insulated from ideas in the outside world, and disproportionately concerned with short-term objectives. This narrowness of outlook is reinforced by the absence in Ireland of any significant movement between private and public employment.

The general pattern of promotion, particularly at higher levels, has been for civil servants to rise within one department. Though in recent years there has been greater mobility between departments in filling top posts, many higher civil servants are set in their thinking as regards their own department's area of specialism. Indeed, it would plainly be difficult to work in a particular area of public policy for most of a career and not develop some firm views. That said, the 'departmental line' is obviously tempered by current political realities; yet it remains an underlying theme in terms of the advice which departmental civil servants offer and provides a certain amount of internal cohesion to them as a group. As regards the administrative elite as a whole, there is a less distinctive but nonetheless important commonality of approach, which rests on a sense of its own indispensability, corporate responsibility and self-interest.

The administrative elite works in a system the main organisational characteristics of which were inherited from Britain. In Ireland, however, the elite is not marked out by social distance from other public servants. There is no tradition of social exclusivity. The main barrier to entry into the public service is educational achievement, which in Ireland has been eased for almost all classes by free or inexpensive secondary schooling. There is an inevitable tendency for higher civil servants to have attended schools run by religious orders, given the traditional reliance on clerically provided secondary education; but there is no 'old school tie' tradition, as there is in Britain.

As in so many other European countries, only in recent years have women begun to figure at a senior level among the administrative elite. Despite 64 per cent of civil servants being women, female representation at the senior levels is low. Indeed, it would seem that while outnumbered at the junior levels, men are increasingly over-represented in higher posts. Thus, for illustration, in 1997 there were 303 male Principal Officers, compared with forty-one women in the same grade. Of ninety-eight Assistant Secretaries, only ten were women.

The administrative elite, then, is not marked out educationally, culturally or socially from other Irish elites, even though senior civil servants are a particularly powerful group. They operate at the core of the highly centralised, secretive, self-protective, pervasive and unrivalled administrative machine outlined in Chapter 4. None of the other elites bring the same level of sustained, informed and rigorous attention to any public issue as can the administrative elite.

The most senior public servants at local government level are the County or City Managers and they too deserve mention here. These Managers are also powerful, but are less shielded from public criticism, because they are more publicly accountable for their actions and advice. City and County Managers are also further from the key legislative processes. But despite the fact that they remain to some degree subservient to central government, they do have a substantial degree of autonomy from their own local politicians and are clearly at the hub of the local administration. Indeed, while the approximate equivalents of local government managers employed by the health boards administer major services on behalf of the community, they are even more clearly subordinate to Dublin. Socially and educationally, however, all these administrators are from similar backgrounds to civil servants – perhaps the most important difference being that City and County Managers will tend to have served in several parts of the country.

One common feature of the Irish administrative elite is a high level of self-conscious nationalism. This attitude is a product both of Ireland's comparatively recent independent status and of its proximity to a much more powerful and older state. In part this nationalism is expressed in the support given to the Irish language, as a symbol of identity and separateness. More importantly, however, it is reflected in the elite's positive attitudes to economic development and relative lack of concern about environmental and social disruption. The elite's outlook as regards such development gives the representatives of economic interest groups an important 'insider' status in the formulation of public policy. It also fashions the terms of public discussion and gives an advantage to those who can present their private interests as being congruent with the national interest.

Interest groups and social partnership

The major economic interest groups – employers, trade unions and farming organisations – have in recent years come to be described as 'social partners' with government. Their participation in policy formulation is formalised in numerous advisory and consultative bodies, such as the National Economic and Social Council (NESC). In October 1987 the social partners arrived at what can now be seen as a watershed agreement, the Programme for National Recovery (PNR). In essence, it dictated the level of pay rises, taxation and social benefits, as well as the extent of public investment in education, housing and job creation for a period three years.[5]

That the PNR was but the beginning of a pattern of success was marked by the achievement of four similar, successive, agreements: the 1991 Programme for Economic and Social Progress (PESP); the 1994 Programme for Competitiveness and Work (PCW); the 1997 Partnership 2000 (P2000); and, most recently, the Programme for Prosperity and Fairness (PPF), negotiated in 2000. During this period social partnership was widened to include the agricultural sector as well as community and voluntary groups – the so-called 'social pillar'.

Like all its predecessors, the PPF has not been without its problems and, as a result of much higher than expected price increases, a renegotiation of the pay aspect of the agreement was completed in early 2001. This has provoked some critics to question whether the partnership model retains its usefulness in the face of both inflation and the continuation of significant social inequalities. Support from the government, all the main political parties and the major interest groups for this highly corporatist approach to economic and industrial relations management remains strong, nonetheless; and the undoubted consensus is that social partnership has been essential to the sustained period of economic growth which Ireland has enjoyed in the recent 'Celtic Tiger' years. As former Taoiseach Garret FitzGerald judges it:

> There can be no doubt about the contribution that successive national partnership agreements have made to our economic and social progress. Much of the spectacular economic growth we have achieved has been due to the basic trade-off in these agreements between personal tax cuts and pay moderation.... [S]uccessive agreements have included many other provisions extending over the whole range of social policies.... The exceptionally wide range and detail of the social issues addressed are in part a reflection of the fact that the community and voluntary sector of our society has in recent years been involved as a full partner in this negotiating process.[6]

Employers and trade unions

Aside from government, the two main groups involved in the negotiation of this succession of agreements have been the Irish Business and Employers' Confederation (IBEC) and the Irish Congress of Trade Unions (ICTU). IBEC was formed in 1992 by a merger of the Confederation of Irish Industry and the Federated Union of Employers. It represents more than 4,000 companies and organisations in all sectors of economic and commercial activity. Funded by subscriptions and fees, it provides economic data and analysis for its members and represents business interests in negotiations with the trade unions and government. Through its Brussels office, the Irish Business Bureau, it also works on behalf of business and employers at EU level.

The influence of multinational companies in Ireland has led some commentators to predict a decline in the role of IBEC. The argument is that IBEC's main role is as a corporatist social partner. But since multinationals are controlled by global considerations, they might not be inclined to join and support an organisation which requires them to accord with a policy on, for example, employee remuneration which is in conflict with the policy of their own corporate headquarters. Despite this argument, most large foreign firms have adopted a 'when in Rome' policy as regards local business practice and have been fully supportive of IBEC and its lobbying activities.

The other major social partner is the trade union movement. Despite the nationalist/republican inclinations of James Connolly, James Larkin and the other towering figures in the Irish labour tradition in the second decade of the twentieth century, the trade union movement in Ireland has, by and large, stood aside from involvement in the national question. Connolly's vision went beyond the purely nationalist struggle. He argued that freedom from Britain was only a part of the greater struggle for freedom from the capitalist system. As Connolly put it:

If you remove the English army tomorrow and hoist the green flag over Dublin Castle, unless you set about the organisation of the Socialist Republic your efforts would be in vain![7]

Larkin, in keeping with his essentially syndicalist view, saw the unions as the key mechanism in advancing the achievement of a socialist organisation of society. However, following the defeat of the unions in the great 1913 Dublin lockout, Larkin went to America (where he was jailed for subversion) and did not return until after independence; and Connolly was shot for his part in the Easter Rising.

The new leadership of the Irish Trade Union Congress (ITUC) had a more restricted view of the political role of the workers, as regards both the developing independence struggle and the pursuit of socialism. Partition was, of course, a problem for the trade unions, but more for institutional than for political reasons. The ITUC remained intact as the trade union centre for the whole of Ireland, but many of its affiliated unions were British-based and continued to organise in the Free State. After independence, therefore, tensions between the new and growing Irish-based unions and the long-established British unions were inevitable. There came to be a particular enmity between the two largest organisations – the Irish Transport and General Workers' Union (ITGWU) and the British-based Amalgamated Transport and General Workers' Union (ATGWU). This culminated in 1944 in the breakaway from the ITUC of the ITGWU and seventeen other Irish-based unions to form the Congress of Irish Unions (CIU). Despite constant efforts to heal the breach, the CIU and the ITUC remained apart until 1959, when they finally merged to create the ICTU.

The ICTU today has sixty-three affiliated trade unions, representing around 660,000 workers, of whom roughly 450,000 are in the Republic (in sixty or so unions) and 210,000 in Northern Ireland (in just over forty unions); there are eighteen unions with members in both the Republic and Northern Ireland. The three largest unions until the early 1990s were the ITGWU, the ATGWU and the Federated Workers' Union of Ireland (FWUI), which together held the great majority of members. Those few unions not affiliated to the ICTU represent around 10 per cent (or 70,000) of unionised workers. Union membership in the Republic, as a proportion of people in work, is relatively stable (over 45 per cent – as compared with less than 30 per cent in Britain).

There have recently been some important union mergers, designed mainly to achieve economies of scale and, hopefully, a better service to members. In

1990 the ITGWU and the FWUI joined forces to form the Services, Industrial, Professional, Technical Union (SIPTU), which has well over 200,000 members. Similarly, the bodies representing many local government and civil service employees are now merged in a union called IMPACT, which has a membership of around 35,000.

The ICTU has no formal position on partition, except to the extent that it has always insisted that there must be no change in the status of Northern Ireland without the consent of the people there. Associated with that, it has also been among the strongest opponents of the use of violence for political purposes. As for the party politics of the Republic, the ICTU tends towards a non-partisan position, perhaps in the knowledge that Fianna Fáil has always attracted more of the working-class vote than the Labour Party. Despite the continuing reservations of some of its major affiliates, the ICTU has been a steady supporter of the centralised, corporatist agreements such as the PPF.

The farmers

Land has traditionally held an important position for Irish people. Until the 1930s it was seen as the lifeblood of the economy and it still makes a major contribution to the wealth of the country. But land and the people who work it have long been regarded as much more than economic assets. The ownership of land is charged with much social, political and cultural significance. The model of the family farm remains an important part of Ireland's self-image. The transfer of ownership effected in the late nineteenth century means that now more than 90 per cent of Irish farmers own their land.

The Irish Creamery Milk Suppliers' Association (ICMSA), one of the two largest farming organisations, was founded in 1950 to campaign on behalf of farmers who produced milk. The bulk of milk production used to come from small farms, but this pattern has now changed, with 12 per cent of suppliers providing 40 per cent of the milk sent to creameries. The number of milk suppliers has reduced in recent years and now stands at about 58,000. The ICMSA has, therefore, had to broaden its appeal. It was formerly a very militant organisation and in 1953 called a successful sixteen-day strike in support of its demand for an increase in the price paid to farmers for their milk. But within a few years the ICMSA came to be regarded as fairly conservative. It believes in intensification of agricultural production on small farms; and it is suspicious of land reform and of EU programmes for modernisation and the retirement of elderly farmers. The ICMSA has its headquarters in Limerick and organises its 52,000 members through 480 branches across the country.

The main farming organisation, however, is the Irish Farmers' Association (IFA). The IFA grew out of the National Farmers' Association, which was set up in 1955. It developed into a highly efficient body and employed agricultural experts to present its case to government for improvements in farming and farm incomes. By the mid-1960s the IFA was recognised by government as the farmers' representative, to be consulted regularly on the formulation of agricultural policy. The IFA was very militant in the 1960s, reflecting farmers' anger at their economic difficulties. There was the feeling among the farming community that it had been left behind by an economic plan that concentrated on the development of an Irish industrial sector. During the militant campaigns of the 1960s, farmers went to gaol as a result of protests. Today, the IFA is much more integrated into the national policy-making system. With a membership of over 150,000, many regard it as Ireland's most effective interest group. For example, well before Irish entry to the EU, the IFA had opened an office in Brussels.

Two further organisations are also an important part of the farm lobby. The Irish Co-operative Organisation articulates the views of a crucial section of the fast-growing food industry. Its voice is of increasing importance because of major restructuring in recent years. Macra na Feirme (the Young Farmers' Association) lobbies on behalf of young farmers on such issues as inheritance taxes and agricultural education. It has over 10,000 members and many powerful figures in agricultural politics are former members.

The greatest overall improvement for Irish agriculture came with entry to the EU. As well as bringing higher and guaranteed prices, the EU has attempted to modernise farming, by encouraging the enlargement of farms, the use of better technology and the education of farmers. Though the number of small farms (under thirty acres) has declined, the rate of decline has been much slower than many expected. There has also been much less stress on the frugality, spirituality and cosiness of rural life as envisaged by Eamon de Valera. The political, administrative and agricultural elites agree on the need to ensure the competitiveness of the upper-income farmers; on the necessity to retain or achieve viability for the middle-income group; and on the import-ance of addressing the problems of current low earners, through social policy and encouragement of mobility of land ownership.

The Catholic Church

One powerful force in Ireland that has had, and continues to have, a major influence on Irish society is the Roman Catholic Church. In 1911, almost 90 per cent of the population of the twenty-six counties which were to make up the Irish Free State were Catholics. This figure has increased to over 95 per cent at present. The proportion of committed and practising Catholics in Ireland marks it off from other EU countries with large Catholic populations.

Before independence, government in Ireland was a predominantly Prot-estant business. The Catholic Church supported the nationalist movement and kept its distance from the government. After independence this aloofness was maintained. In other countries conflict arises between church and state because the church wishes to extend, maintain or defend its influence in the face of increased state activity. In the Free State, there was no major driving force for the secularisation of the new state. Some influential and senior clerics urged Irish governments to enact distinctly Catholic legislation. At the same time, there was no general desire on the Church's part to extend its authority, because it was satisfied with the influence it already had.

In respect of social welfare services, for instance, the Church has a stake that might seem extensive to visitors from Protestant countries. The state does not attempt to provide all such services itself and many hospitals, orphanages, juvenile reformatories and other welfare institutions are run by Catholic religious orders, with the aid of government grants and, to varying extents, under government control. The interpenetration of church and state is seen most clearly in the field of education. Education is not merely denominationally controlled: it is clerically controlled.[8]

In the conclusion of his definitive study, Whyte looks at two opposing propositions on the influence of the Catholic Church in Ireland. On the one hand, he disagrees with the assertion that Ireland is a theocratic state 'in which the hierarchy has the final say on any matter in which it wishes to intervene'. In his view, the total record does not show that Irish governments 'have automatically deferred to the hierarchy on any point on which the hierarchy chooses to speak'.[9] On the other hand, he feels that the notion that the Church is only one among a number of interest groups in society is naive. For in the final analysis, in a mainly Catholic country, the Catholic hierarchy has a weapon that no other group possesses: its authority over people's consciences. Most politicians are practising Catholics and accept the hierarchy's right to speak on matters of faith or morals. Even politicians who are personally indifferent to religion recognise that most of the electorate are believers and will act accordingly.[10]

In the past, the Church's influence had much to do with the social structure in Ireland. This consisted largely of rural communities, where priests found it relatively easy to exercise control over the inhabitants. But the situation has changed decisively because of urbanisation and industrialisation. Urban dwellers and the young are more willing to question established social and moral values, while increased disposable income, foreign travel, newspapers and television have led to an erosion of religiosity in Ireland.

The lessening of the Church's influence has been reflected in changes in the laws governing such issues as the availability of contraceptives, the censorship of books and films and the legalisation of homosexual activity. In 1995 a narrow majority voted in a referendum for the introduction of divorce, despite direct appeals from the Pope and the Irish hierarchy. Moreover, much evidence has accumulated on the widening gap between the attitudes to religion between the old and the young and between those living in Dublin and those outside the capital. By late 1995 many commentators were talking about a 'Church in crisis', with the majority of its members, especially young people, having little or no confidence in Church leaders. The reasons for this rapid decline in respect are complex. Some are connected to developments in Catholicism internationally, such as a conservative papacy and a retreat from the more tolerant tone of the Second Vatican Council. Others are related to a series of revelations of serious sexual misconduct at every level of the clergy and religious orders: priests have been convicted of paedophilia; and a senior bishop was revealed to have a son living in the United States. More broadly, the Catholic Church in Ireland has appeared defensive, secretive and un-welcoming of lay involvement at a time when other aspects of Irish life were becoming much more transparent and participative. As Dr William Walsh put it when speaking to a conference of priests in April 1996:

> there is a perception that we, as bishops and other religious authorities, in-volved ourselves in a web of secrecy that was designed to protect the abuser rather than the abused.... There has been dismay and distress among Catholics at the state of their Church. There has been real grief at the death of their own illusions.[11]

The influence of the Catholic Church over the morals, and especially the sexual morality, of Irish people may have declined, but the Church is still powerful and socially pervasive. Ninety-five per cent of all schools are under Catholic management, as are many social and health facilities. Parish clergy are active in all forms of community, sports and social organisations, especially in rural areas. Nuns are to the forefront in many campaigns for social justice. And the Church is involved in many aspects of Irish public life which in other countries are usually the exclusive province of secular authorities.

Finally, demonstrating that the hierarchy is far from being the only source of pressure on the state to support Catholic values, there has been a remark-able increase in lobbying and pressure group activity led by lay people. Furthermore, organisations such as the Society for the Protection of the Unborn Child (SPUC) and the Pro-Life Amendment Campaign (PLAC) have shown that Catholic opinion in Ireland can still be mobilised into a powerful lobby on moral questions. This been particularly evident at times when governmental majorities have been slender.

The media

Arguably not quite an elite, still less a pressure group in the normally accepted sense, journalists in Ireland certainly *seek* to have an influence on the politics of the nation. Until the 1930s, there were just two main national daily papers. The *Irish Times*, the voice of Irish Unionism before independence, became, and remains, non-party. As Ireland's daily 'paper of record', it claims – with some justice – to produce both the most serious and the most radical journalism in the Republic; it is run by a trust and has a specific brief to advance the cause of a pluralist and more liberal Ireland. The *Irish Independent* and its evening and Sunday sisters are also at the quality end of the market by international standards; supporters of Cumann na nGaedheal during the early years of independence, they are now less uncritical in their backing of its successor, Fine Gael – and frequently espouse 'new right' thinking, especially on the economy.

The lack of a newspaper supporting Fianna Fáil led de Valera to set up the *Irish Press* soon after his party first came to power in the 1930s. It quickly became the most popular paper in Ireland and led the market for nearly fifty years. However, in the 1980s the *Irish Press* and its evening and Sunday stablemates not only became less closely identified with Fianna Fáil (despite remaining in the hands of the de Valera family), but also fell on hard times. The group was the subject of several rescue attempts, but finally expired in 1995 – occasioning considerable shock and dismay, even among its rivals.

The morning national press now consists of four main papers: the two remaining traditional dailies; the *Irish Star*, a less sensational version of the British paper of the same name (jointly owned by the British Express and the Irish Independent groups); and the successful non-aligned Cork-based paper, the *Irish Examiner*. Sunday offers a wider choice, including a colourful tabloid specialising in scandal and a specialist business broadsheet.

There is also a lively, and often highly political, weekly provincial press in Ireland, meshing neatly with the concern of so many politicians with parish-pump issues. At the same time, there are considerable worries about the penetration into Ireland of British newspapers – the tabloids in particular – which sometimes cost less than half the price of their Irish counterparts.

Irish newspapers and broadcasting are notable for their restraint in reporting on the personal lives of people in the public eye, especially politicians. There is – almost as a consequence – one serious blot on the media's escutcheon. It relates to the virtual immunity from close scrutiny of the private and public conduct over the years of Charles Haughey, the former leader of Fianna Fáil. Now seriously discredited as a result of revelations of financial misdeeds (see Chapter 6), Haughey adopted over the years what he has himself described as a 'don't complain and don't explain' strategy. The result was that the media stopped asking questions about how he maintained his ostentatiously expensive lifestyle and the conspicuous consumption associated with it. Had they done so, it seems unlikely that it would have taken so long for the truth to emerge.

But like the free press everywhere, newspapers in Ireland have frequently been the progenitors of major policy change, especially as a consequence of good investigative journalism. The same has been true of Irish radio and television. Radio Telefís Éireann (RTÉ) is the state broadcasting organisation; it is responsible for three television and four radio channels and has been joined during the last decade by a mushrooming independent radio sector. Although

RTÉ (like the BBC in Britain and national public broadcasting stations in the United States) is legally required to be politically non-partisan, it has been a significant force for social and, it follows, political change. RTÉ's most recent broadcasting venture, set up in 1996, was Teilifís na Gaeilge, an Irish-language television station, since renamed TG4. However, TV3, the third national television network, broke RTÉ's Irish television monopoly in 1998 and is steadily building an audience. TV3 is part owned by Granada Media, the dominant player in Britain's independent television sector. Indeed, what makes the job of Irish television particularly difficult in competitive terms is that all the main British television channels are also available virtually all over the country.

It is notoriously difficult to measure the influence of the press, radio and television on public opinion, still more to gauge the effect that they have in convincing politicians that change is necessary in this or that area of national life. It is nonetheless impossible to deny that free and independent media are crucial components of a modern democracy. In this respect, Ireland seems well served.

Conclusion

The structure and distribution of power in Ireland are similar to those in other liberal democratic states. Although Ireland is, in formal terms, a meritocratic country, upward social mobility is restricted. As in other capitalist countries, the most powerful interest groups in Ireland are those concerned with the economy. Employers' organisations accept the state's management of the economy along free market lines; and employees' organisations offer no strong challenge to the broadly capitalist development of Ireland – the trade unions being essentially concerned with defending workers against low pay, poor working conditions and unemployment. The economic, administrative and political elites share a common attachment to an essentially developmental image of the direction in which Ireland is moving – and they are not as distant from the general population as elites in many other countries. The media, too, are part of this consensus, but can be among the most influential, if intermittent, forces for change.

There are many interest groups in Ireland not directly concerned with the economy. Several have existed for some time and campaign on cultural issues such as the preservation of the Irish language and traditions and the promotion of uniquely Irish sports. In recent years several campaigning groups have grown up to press their views on specific issues, such as military neutrality and combating poverty. Other 'one-issue' campaigns, such as the remarkable push in 1988 against the introduction of the requirement for a licence to go fishing, bring previously non-political groups into public controversy – but only for a short time. Similarly, environmental groups or those concerned to protect Ireland's architectural heritage are occasionally brought to the fore because of some issue that captures the general public's imagination. The non-economic organisation with the strongest influence in Ireland remains, however, the Roman Catholic Church.

Interest groups press their views on public policy through a variety of methods. Usually the most effective are those groups whose views are heard away from the public gaze – those inside the policy 'community' which is dominated by ministers and civil servants. Street protests may show numerical strength or deep conviction, but they often signal a real lack of influence on the formation of public policy.

Notes

1 G. Parry, *Political Elites,* London: Allen & Unwin, 1967, p. 13.
2 Department of Finance, *Ireland: National Development Plan 2000–2006,* Dublin: Government Publications Office, 1999, pp. 187–8.
3 C. Whelan and B. Whelan, *Social Mobility in the Republic of Ireland: A Comparative Perspective,* Dublin: Economic and Social Research Institute, 1984, p. 3.
4 P. Clancy and J. Wall, *Social Background of Higher Education Entrants,* Dublin: Higher Education Authority, 2000.
5 See T. Cradden, 'Social partnership in Ireland – against the trend', in N. Collins (ed.), *Political Issues in Ireland Today,* 2nd edition, Manchester: Manchester University Press, 1999.
6 *Irish Times,* 12 February 2000.
7 J. P. Berresford-Ellis, *James Connolly: Selected Writings,* Harmondsworth: Penguin, 1981, p. 124.
8 J. H. Whyte, *Church and State in Modern Ireland, 1923–79,* Dublin: Gill & Macmillan, 1971, pp. 16–17.
9 *Ibid.,* p. 369.
10 *Ibid.,* p. 368.
11 Quoted in the *Irish Times,* 23 April 1996.

Further reading

Breen, R., Hannan, D., Rottman, D. and Whelan, C. *Understanding Contemporary Ireland,* Dublin: Gill & Macmillan, 1990.
Clancy, P., Drudy, S., Lynch, K. and O'Dowd, L. (eds), *Irish Society: A Sociological Perspective,* Dublin: Institute of Public Administration, 1995.

4

The policy-making process

Public policies are the products of government. They take many forms. Some follow public announcements made with much fanfare in the context of lively public debate. Others evolve from the practice of government, that is what civil servants, police officers, teachers and others in authority actually do. Indeed, in many areas of public policy there is a considerable gap between what is formally declared to be policy and what actually happens. This is because the process of making policy is much more complex than is conventionally understood. Those most closely involved – ministers, civil servants and other public officials – may actually contribute to this misunderstanding. They often suggest that the process consists of the politicians deciding policy, while bureaucrats simply administer or carry out their decisions. In this way, citizens are reassured that only those actors who are democratically accountable to the electorate are responsible for the allocation of scarce public resources. The electorate and the media reinforce this politician-centred model. They also focus too much attention on the most obvious characters in the political drama: the Taoiseach and his (it is not yet possible to say 'her') ministers, as well as their leading parliamentary opponents.

In this chapter, policy is taken to be what government does rather than simply what is formally described as policy. It is the cumulative impact of laws, rules, orders, incentives and the use of discretion by those in authority, whether they are elected or not. In Ireland, for reasons of electoral pressure and public expectation, many politicians present themselves as able to alter, in individual cases, what central or local government does. Thus, some citizens believe that public policy is the result of endless interventions by politicians in the operation of government departments, local authorities and other public bodies. The Department of Social Welfare, for example, deals with 40,000 representations and approaching 5,000 parliamentary questions per year about its day-to-day operations. Explanations of public policy-making that concentrate on the brokerage activities of politicians are interesting, but mostly because of what they reveal about elections. They are hardly adequate.

however, to explain the vast majority of either decisions in which politicians play no direct part or, more importantly, the decisions that transcend particular individual interests. In this chapter, the process by which major public decisions, such as hospital closures or infrastructural investments, are made is examined. How the public service is organised to deal with such decisions is central to the process.

External influences on policy

The Republic has undergone numerous important changes of policy direction, especially since the late 1950s. A long period of protectionism in economic policy, parity between the Irish pound (called 'punt' in the Irish language) and sterling and the near-total dependence on the UK market has ended. By 1985, more goods were being exported to the continental EU states than to the UK. In 2000, the United States had become Ireland's largest export market, taking IR£10.9 billion worth of goods and services or more than half of all exports to non-EU countries. As a result, the state's trade agency, Forfás, was warning that Ireland's strong dependence on the United States and – to a lesser extent – the UK made it vulnerable to the fluctuation of the euro against the dollar and sterling. Ireland's economic policies will reflect these new circumstances and other related social, cultural and environmental choices will undoubtedly present themselves.

So whose ideas fashioned these major national decisions – who sets the policy process in train? One answer, which might be drawn from the discussion in Chapter 1, might be 'nobody in Ireland'! Certainly, as a small state relying on international trade and multinational companies, decisions made in Chicago, London, Tokyo and elsewhere can have an immediate impact in Ireland. Even a decision to place new investment or orders in other countries with similar levels of development can have a direct impact on Irish public policy. Often such decisions are taken without reference to Ireland at all, but are made for reasons of global commercial strategy. Nevertheless, patterns of employment, education and social expenditure in the Republic are directly affected. Thus, the decision to move a manufacturing operation to Spain may mean more emigration from the west of Ireland, with resultant changes in school, medical and other provision. No Irish voice needs to be heard, at least until the decision on which of County Mayo's schools or hospital wards is to close is forced on politicians or public servants by changed demography. Some outside accidents or chance events – such as the Chernobyl nuclear meltdown, which contaminated sheep on mountain farms in Ireland – may also have a long-term impact of an unpredictable nature. To an extent, therefore, policy decisions represent reactions to outside pressures.

Of course, Ireland is not simply a recipient of outside influences, important though they are. Even in relation to multinational investment, public bodies –

such as the Industrial Development Authority (IDA) – examine, encourage, promote and decline offers of commercial developments. Increasingly, misgivings about the environmental impact of proposed investments are cited when foreign companies are spurned. Nevertheless, most of the time, the Republic's economy is open to outside as well as domestic investment initiatives. Many decisions in Irish public policy are in effect conditioned by this reality.

'Great man' policy-making

To recognise the importance of outside influence is not to ignore autonomous Irish action. Not everyone would see the Republic's current economic status or its social policies as primarily predetermined. For example, Ireland did not *have* to borrow money to support public spending when the oil crisis of the mid-1970s radically upset the world economy. The role of Irish actors must therefore be assessed. The shift of emphasis in Ireland's political and social policies since the late 1950s is popularly explained by the impact of a senior civil servant, T. K. Whitaker, and the then Taoiseach, Seán Lemass. The two men are credited with formulating, popularising and forming a coalition of support for a dramatic policy with new laws, innovative institutions and fresh thinking about economics, planning and development.

'Great men' do, therefore, have some impact on the policy process, but their scope for innovation is limited by important political, economic and social considerations. Lemass, for example, had been a senior minister for many years in administrations of a conservative and protectionist kind. His espousal of radical measures on free trade, planning and Northern Ireland must be seen in the light of economic crisis, high emigration and pressure on his party's popularity. Fianna Fáil needed to react to the symptoms of a national malaise that threatened its legitimacy as 'the national party'. Further, Lemass' ideas drew directly on European and Christian social principles. His administrations were, in part, the Irish vehicle for a European-wide set of ideas fashionable among Christian Democrats. Whitaker was only one of a group of civil servants challenging the received wisdom of his civil service department.

The policy process is an interaction between ideas, social and political pressures and opportunity in the context of the world economic order. The popularity of the 'great man' explanation of the policy process arises from the simplification and dramatisation it allows in our understanding of events. In fact, the process is far more mundane, complex and unsatisfactory. It involves many people and agencies marching to tunes of self-interest, with remarkably little common purpose. In Ireland, most of the important participants in the making of major national decisions belong to the higher levels of the government bureaucracy, economic pressure groups, major companies and senior politicians.

'Professionals' and the bureaucracy

The number of people involved in policy-making at the highest level may actually be less than 500. The assertion earlier that policy is what government does should, however, alert us to the significance of decisions made, and discretion exercised, by even the lowliest public official. Formal declarations of non-discrimination against travelling people, for example, are not real descriptions of policy if Gardaí (police officers) regularly harass such people, or housing offices routinely ignore their plight. The Beef Tribunal that reported in 1994 looked into allegations of irregularities under the Export Credit Guarantee Insurance Scheme in respect of beef exports in 1987–88. In doing so, it highlighted major gaps between formal policy and administrative practice.

The government bureaucracy includes many public servants who prefer to be seen as professionals rather than bureaucrats. 'Professionals' frequently claim that their judgements are based on abstract and neutral ideas, and are to that extent non-political. Thus, health policy relies in part on the pattern of priorities advocated by health board doctors and not just on instructions from the Department of Health. When questioned about their decisions, doctors regularly talk of 'clinical judgement'. The scarce resources that they command – such as medicines and operating theatres – should, it is thus claimed, be outside the public arena, because only his or her peers can judge a doctor's priorities. Though their use of resources for one treatment may deny them for another, doctors, like engineers and other professionals, would not regard themselves as part of a *political* process. Further, though governments set the total spending limits, the precise allocation of funds to different hospitals and specialisms has been devolved to local health board members. Boards of councillors, medical and paramedical professionals and ministerial appointees, therefore, significantly influence health policy.

Government departments and their civil servants

In this chapter, we will be concentrating on major decisions. In Ireland, these are largely the outcome of initiatives taken within government departments. Where legislation is required to enforce new policies, the government's majority in the legislature secures this. All the main parties run on tightly authoritarian lines and Irish governments can usually retain control, despite small majorities – or even when in a minority – if the opposition is divided.

Government departments are organised on functional lines to cover the major areas of policy, such as agriculture, health and foreign affairs. The main Irish government departments are:

- Department of An Taoiseach;
- Department of Finance;
- Department of Agriculture and Food;

- Department of Arts, Heritage, Gaeltacht and the Islands;
- Department of Defence;
- Department of Education;
- Department of Enterprise, Trade and Employment;
- Department of the Environment and Local Government;
- Department of Foreign Affairs;
- Department of Health and Children;
- Department of Justice, Equality and Law Reform;
- Department of the Marine and Natural Resources;
- Department of Social, Community and Family Affairs;
- Department of Tourism, Sport and Recreation;
- Department of Public Enterprise.

The administrative cost of running departments, as opposed to expenditure on the provision of the services for which they are responsible, is about 10 per cent of total government spending. There are over thirty departments, or equivalents, but the Department of Finance occupies an essential position, as the custodian of government money. Each department is staffed by civil servants, the most senior of whom is called the Secretary General. Departmental Secretaries General, their Assistant Secretaries and Principal Officers are the most powerful public servants in the government bureaucracy. Their ideas of what is desirable, possible and, to a degree, politically advantageous for the government are most influential in deciding what is done. The Secretaries General are the main channels of civil service advice available to ministers and, though ministers frequently change, their advisers do not. Because of their influence, much attention has been focused by critics on what is claimed to be their lack of social vision and openness to new ideas. Such comments have often centred on their supposedly narrow educational background and their cautious outlook, encouraged by slow promotion and lack of experience of work in the private sector.

All but one of the twenty-three Secretaries General in 2001 were men. They normally hold office for a maximum of seven years. Some observers have suggested that continuation in their appointments should be linked to their performance. In this way, they would have an extra incentive to impose more accountable management systems on their departments. Traditionally, once appointed, Secretaries General were very secure in their posts. Their career paths have typically been entirely within the civil service. Though the top posts are now open to wider competition, *de facto* most appointments are by internal promotion.

Those in the senior ranks below Secretary General may have entered the service after university, but still at a junior grade. Civil servants themselves see that the hierarchical system has some dampening effect on initiative but feel that caution, even parsimony, is a virtue in a servant of the public. Though some management techniques may have been learned from the private sector, the civil servants' view of the world is distinctive. Public service, in the opinion of senior civil servants, remains a bastion of integrity, national responsibility and hard work, which bears laudable comparison to other sectors of Irish public life. As a former Secretary General of the Department of An Taioseach put it:

> I am proud that the Irish civil service ... has a record in providing quality services that compares well with the civil services of other countries ... and with any of the private organisations I have encountered.[1]

It is indeed difficult to argue with such a view. It may be, however, that this self-image makes senior civil servants somewhat unresponsive to new ideas from business, academia, pressure groups and elsewhere.

Parties and policy-making – sidelining the civil service?

The exact list of tasks carried out by, and the title of, each government department varies with changing political fashion and administrative convenience. There remains, however, a fairly identifiable core of departments which have been involved with agriculture, defence, education, local government, foreign affairs and other major areas since the early years of the state. It would be odd if, as individuals and collectively, public officials who worked in these areas did not develop coherent and generalised views of where the public interest lies. Even modest, self-effacing civil servants would presumably make at least some effort to resist serious challenges to the 'departmental line' from their nominal superiors – government ministers. Of course, ministers ultimately have to prevail if open clashes of opinion occur. Plainly, senior politicians also have their own ideas about public priorities, particularly in relation to major policy initiatives.

When a single party forms a government, its ideas may be fairly broad and open to change through Cabinet reconsideration and civil service advice. In a coalition, however, some distinct policy ideas may have been decided by prior negotiation between the parties. Subsequent civil service reservations may therefore count for little. To ensure a coalition survives, individual ministers may view it as their primary task to 'deliver' on a policy promise, despite reservations from within their own party or department. When the 1973 Fine Gael/ Labour coalition was formed, several Labour ministers appointed advisers from outside the civil service to provide them with non-departmental advice. This practice has since been adopted to varying degrees by subsequent governments.

Since 1992, new coalition governments have also appointed 'programme managers', generally from outside the civil service, to monitor the achievement of agreed policy objectives. These managers meet weekly before Cabinet meetings and fulfil a valuable coordinating role between departments. Despite early reservations, most senior civil servants now see the managers, generally one per minister, as an asset. In particular, they help keep the minister in touch with party political opinion, with other ministers and with outside interests; and they are considered to be especially valuable in departments with a reforming agenda. In opposition, Fine Gael was critical of the role of advisers to the Fianna Fáil/Labour government. Nevertheless, John Bruton as Taoiseach continued the system. Indeed, the programme managers were credited with ensuring the relatively low level of friction in the three-party government, despite its broad ideological span. Since programme managers and other political advisers are essentially the personal appointees of ministers, they forfeit their appointments when their ministers leave office. Despite the fairly general approval that these 'outsiders' now enjoy, for most of the time the policy process is still dominated by civil servants acting within the broad parameters set by the government of the day.

'The minister requests...'

The better a party's preparations while in opposition, or the more specific its proposals, the smaller the role civil servants play in policy formulation. Formally, and importantly in legal terms, the orders, advice and publicly expressed opinions of civil servants are all in the name of the minister. Under the Ministers and Secretaries Act 1924, the minister is the 'corporation sole' of the department. All legal powers are conferred on him or her and used in his or her name. Thus phrases such as 'I am instructed by the minister to...' or 'the minister requests...' appear on documents that the minister may never have seen, or of which she or he is only vaguely aware.

Since the same formal language also appears when the minister is showing a direct personal interest in an area of policy, to the outsider the authority of the document is the same. Senior civil servants communicate not only for their minister by letter but also informally through networks of contacts in every aspect of public life. A retired Secretary General of the Department of Finance has written:

> Only those who have worked close to Ministers have any idea of the many demands on their time. One indication of the limited amount of time which a Minister can devote to the affairs of his Department is the difficulty which the official head of the Department (the Secretary) and his senior colleagues experience in obtaining a meeting with him. Perhaps this difficulty is accentuated in the Department of Finance, whose Minister is subject to unusually varied pressures; it is certainly not a problem of personalities since the difficulty does not vary much with different Ministers.[2]

As they do not personally build houses, teach children or manufacture goods, civil servants must keep a check on public policy by monitoring those who do. Information is crucial and the skill of interpreting it central to the civil servants' role. For this reason their work is dominated by a stream of official figures, reports from their juniors, personal impressions, politicians' and citizens' letters, gossip and media speculation. Their centrality in these networks of information is both a strength and a source of vulnerability for civil servants. How do they make sense of it all? The model of the world they employ is a vitally important element in how policy is formed and reformed. This is why the departmental line, the civil servants' backgrounds and the openness to fresh ideas are important.

Keeping track of policy

There is a constitutional limit of fifteen on the number of Cabinet ministers and they may be assisted by up to seventeen ministers of state. All must be members of the Oireachtas (two may be from the Seanad). To form an idea of how difficult it is for ministers to keep track of the areas of policy for which they are responsible, it is useful to look at the structure of even a small department. The primary functions of the Department of Foreign Affairs are to advise the government on Ireland's external relations, to be a channel for official communications with foreign governments and international agencies; and to monitor developments in Northern Ireland. EU business is a significant burden for the Department. Yet despite all this, its running costs, at home and abroad, account for less than 0.5 per cent of total government expenditure. About 130 people above the level of Third Secretary (the 'first rung' diplomatic grade within the Department of Foreign Affairs staffing structure) are based in headquarters in Dublin. Several hundred more employees, many of them not Irish, are dispersed in various forms of official representation around the world. Forty-eight per cent of the Department's staff is engaged in overseas assignments. In 2001, there were over fifty separate embassies, consulates and their equivalents situated abroad.

It would be unreasonable to expect ministers to be *au fait* with all of their department's work. Nevertheless, any task is liable to become the focus of public controversy. Thus, for example, the routine issuing of passports, to which few ministers had given much attention, became a political embarrassment in 1987, when irregularities were discovered to be occurring at the Irish Embassy in London. Although these seemed to be attributable to a specific civil servant, the Minister for Foreign Affairs was called on to give an account of how such a situation 'was allowed to happen'.

More important for policy-making is the rivalry that exists between departments. Thus, to take another Foreign Affairs example, EU matters have been the responsibility of that Department since the negotiations for Ireland's entry in 1973. Nevertheless, the Department's views, tutored by the exigencies of diplomacy, can be brought to fruition only if they prevail over the possibly conflicting views of those responsible for Finance and Agriculture. To some extent, departments 'capture' areas of discretion or advice. If responsibility is given to another department, control over the flow of information, prestige and power are lost. Thus, there might just be conflict between the Department of Foreign Affairs and the Department of Enterprise, Trade and Employment concerning negotiations on trade treaties with foreign governments or international organisations.

In many government departments it is difficult to assess the impact of policy other than in terms of increased service provision. Whether, as a consequence, Ireland is better educated, defended, housed or provided for in terms of health and welfare is difficult to gauge. A reasonable measure may, however, be what is spent on these services. Thus civil servants who come to identify an increase in their service with the general national good may be motivated to maximise their departmental budgets. Such motives, with the understandable personal interest in more salary, promotion and prestige, have, according to their critics, become significant reasons for the seemingly inexorable growth of public expenditure.

Odium or plaudits for the minister?

Although politicians in government are directly involved in only a small proportion of the policy for which they are 'responsible', that proportion is often the most controversial. The public odium that attends failure, or indeed insensitivity in policy implementation, descends on the politicians in office. Cabinet ministers are especially vulnerable to criticism. By contrast, they must also be seen to receive the plaudits for policy successes and popular initiatives. There are few more prized opportunities for a politician than the opening of a factory, a new road or a hospital in or near his or her constituency. A department that fails to alert its minister to a possibly embarrassing development, or to a potential opportunity to be associated with a success, would be open to sharp criticism. On the other hand, departments rely on their ministers to secure their position in the interdepartmental rivalry on policies and responsibilities. To a civil service department, a good minister wins battles in Cabinet or elsewhere, makes decisions on the files sent to him or her and stands up for the officials in times of criticism. For a minister, a good department is one where the opportunities for good publicity are substantial. Briefly, if the public mood is sympathetic, a minister may even gain in popularity by being seen to take 'unpopular' decisions. The public tolerance for cutbacks is short, however.

Policy or administration?

The supposed dichotomy between policy and administration is one to which civil servants often point. They claim that, once ministers make broad and clearly political choices, they merely facilitate their implementation. To this extent, civil servants are politically neutral administrators, while politicians are the effective policy-makers. This model of the policy process is rather like the legal description. Many analysts of the policy process recognise it to be of limited use, but it remains a powerful ideal.

The efficiency of the public sector in general is a vital part of Ireland's national competitiveness in the global market. More recent reforming ideas that have influenced Ireland's public service are associated with the 'new public management' (NPM) school. This body of thought has been significant in many countries. It arises from a neo-liberal critique that portrays the public sector as inherently inefficient, self-serving and inhibiting rational economic strategies. The response in terms of public sector reforms has been to divest the state of commercial assets, to seek private sector solutions to social problems and to introduce business practices to the civil service. Many of these steps have been influenced by reforms in other countries, particularly New Zealand, Australia and Britain. There has, for example, been a move in the financial planning by government departments from a year-to-year to a three-year basis. Other significant moves have included the privatisation of state-sponsored industries (in effect state-owned companies – on which see more below) such as Telecom Éireann, the national telephone company; private/public partnerships have been formed to provide infrastructural projects like roads and bridges; and a civil service reform programme was introduced, known as the Strategic Management Initiative (SMI).

The SMI calls for a strategic approach by civil servants based on the need for better planning and management. It sets out a schedule of change, starting with a strategy statement by each department taking stock and preparing initial plans. The essential tasks are identifying government objectives and client needs. Each department then outlines what steps and strategies it should pursue to achieve its objectives. The strategy statement and subsequent policy documents are meant to encourage a searching self-analysis. In 2001–02, the SMI calls for external evaluations, departmental performance indicators and other forms of assessment. Many civil servants are enthusiastic about the SMI and other related reforms. There are many, however, who are reluctant to adapt to the new regime.

Improving financial planning and budgetary management

The SMI was encouraged by the experience of cutbacks and financial constraint in the late 1980s. Even today, however, departments must set out the cost of continuing policies for the next year and then for the subsequent two years on a 'no-policy-change' basis. In effect, departments are being obliged to signal the cost of policy changes much more clearly. The new system will thus call for greater budgetary discipline from civil servants. It may, on the

other hand, be even tougher on politicians, because it will make it more difficult to effect changes in the short term.

Such tight budgeting involved severe competition for funds and intense
competition between sections within each department. The major rows, however, have usually been between spending departments and the Department
of Finance and these take place during the autumn months, when detailed
submissions are considered. The Department of Finance aggregates the figures
and compares them with the government's capacity to raise taxes or borrow
money at home or abroad. Inevitably, the Department seeks to reduce expenditure by questioning the need for, the details of, or the costings associated
with each department's proposals. After the haggling is over, Finance pub-
lishes details of the proposed expenditure in January. The Minister for Finance
then prepares his (they have all been men) own budgetary proposals that outline how the government intends to raise the money to meet its bills. In recent
years, this has not involved overall tax increases, but the December budgetary
statement is still politically sensitive, either in the context of particular tax
measures or as regards agreements with the social partners.

In assessing the level of taxation, the Department of Finance works closely
with the Revenue Commissioners, who are responsible for its collection. The
Dáil discusses the government's plans, but only rarely are changes made before
the necessary legislation is passed. Once the Cabinet and civil servants, working in confidence, have arrived at a pattern of expenditure and taxation –
involving intense bargaining and compromise – it would be difficult to find
room for significant adjustments. Further, for a government to be unsuccessful
in carrying its budget in a Dáil vote is a cause of serious political embarrassment. Following his budget statement of December 2000, the Minister for
Finance, Charlie McCreevy, was forced into significant changes to measures
he had announced that altered the tax liabilities of women in the labour force.
This debacle significantly weakened his political position. The annual budgetary cycle is completed when the Comptroller and Auditor-General (C&A-G)
and his or her staff audit each department's accounts. The Dáil's Public
Accounts Committee (PAC) goes through the C&A-G's report in great detail
with the 'accounting officer' (usually the Secretary General) of each department. The Committee is usually chaired by an opposition TD, as a defence
against accusations of favouritism for the government party or parties. Following legislation in 1993, the C&A-G's reports now also cover the 'value for
money' being given by government departments and other public agencies.

Who calls the shots?

The Department of Finance's dominant position in the budgetary process is
only part of the reason for its influence. The Department, which is the only
one mentioned in the Constitution, is involved in all aspects of economic

policy and planning. It negotiates Ireland's trade agreements (though this is now largely a role for the EU) and it has responsibility for monetary and banking policy and the like. It does, however, have rivals. The Department of An Taoiseach is an increasingly important part of the policy-making process. The Taoiseach has been a most influential policy-maker from the beginning. He is, after all, the leader of the main government party and is able to choose his colleagues in government – even though this power is somewhat diminished under a coalition arrangement. It is to him that the public look to champion the government's cause and offer leadership. Until 1982, the Department of An Taoiseach remained small and essentially 'non-interventionist'. Under recent holders of the post, however, the Department has grown in size and so too has the scope of its direct responsibility. It provides policy and administrative support on a variety of issues to other departments, depending on the Taoiseach's priorities and, unlike other departments, it does not have a statutorily defined area of responsibility. Significantly, for reform of the policy process, the Department is charged with the promotion of the SMI.

The Taoiseach, like other ministers, may appoint special advisers with a party political background. The Department of An Taoiseach also has a number of junior ministers – or 'Ministers of State' – attached to it, including the government chief whip. Thus, the Taoiseach's team has a crucial hold on the legislative programme and on party discipline. Especially under single-party governments, the Taoiseach has been able to exercise both forceful leadership and close management of the government's overall business. The Department of An Taoiseach is thus potentially the most powerful department of all.

The role of the Taoiseach as Ireland's representative at the European Council has added to the centrality of his Department. Yet the Department of Foreign Affairs has also gained prominence as a consequence of Ireland's EU membership. Ireland's permanent representation in Brussels is dominated by Foreign Affairs, although other departments, particularly Agriculture, are well represented. Because many policies have their origins in the European Commission, a close watching brief is kept, and representations made, by Irish civil servants based in Brussels.

The scope and responsibilities of local government

Irish local government is less powerful and provides fewer services than in most other European countries. There is no recent tradition of local autonomy and an *ultra vires* rule prevents local authorities from broadening their functions beyond those which central government permits to them. At the moment, the list is dominated by housing, roads, water supply, sanitary services, development control and environmental protection. It is likely that the last area will become more significant as public concern with the environment puts pressure on central government. Similarly, for some authorities, libraries and swimming pools may be the focus of increased public demand. In 1996, the government accepted a list of minor administrative tasks, for example most grant applications in the area of housing, as functions that could be devolved to local government. On the other hand, some tasks presently carried out by local government may be removed – as was the provision of health services some years ago.

The term 'local government' has encompassed a varying collection of tasks down through the years (including the upkeep of courthouses, the dipping of sheep against scabs and the settlement of travelling people). Nevertheless, whatever such changes there may have been from time to time, the local authorities themselves have proved fundamentally enduring and they remain a vital part of Irish democracy. It is possible, if a consensus was reached between the main parties at national level, that local government could become significantly more powerful as a service provider.

Local government – the historical background

Local government in Ireland is based upon nineteenth-century British legislation that provided for single-tier urban and two-tier rural government. Following their accounting practices, local government services can be described under the seven headings of: housing and building; road transportation and safety; water supply and sewerage; development incentives and controls; environmental protection; recreation and amenity; and miscellaneous services. Housing (20 per cent), roads (35 per cent) and water and sewerage (11 per cent) account for the bulk of expenditure.

The chief innovations in local government since independence have involved the establishment of a national agency for local government appointments (1926); a concentration of administrative powers in the office of the City or County Manager (1940); and the abolition of the domestic rating system (1978). The major Irish legislation is, in effect, a number of nineteenth-century British statutes, with a time lag; for example, first came the 1888 (British) Local Government Acts and only afterwards the 1898 (Irish) Local Government Acts.

The five major urban authorities, formally called 'county boroughs', cover the larger cities: Dublin, Cork, Limerick, Waterford and Galway. As well as the county borough council called Dublin Corporation, the Dublin area has three county councils: Dún Laoghaire–Rathdown, Fingal and South Dublin. The rest of the country is divided into twenty-five county council areas, some of which have subordinate authorities within them – known as urban district councils (forty-nine) and town commissioners (twenty-six). Each local authority comprises two elements – the elected members (councillors) and a Manager. County boroughs have between fifteen and fifty-two members; county councils range from twenty to forty-eight; and the rest usually have nine members.

The managerial system in local government

The institution of the City or County Manager is the most distinctive and innovative feature of Irish local government. Broadly, the Manager replaced the executive committees of the British system. The Manager 'reports' his or her decisions to the council; its ability to overturn them is limited but somewhat controversial – as we shall see. The management system was intended mainly to bring about efficient and honest local administration. The period of civil turmoil leading up to 1922 had seen a decline in standards of administration and accounting. Cumann na nGaedheal governments acted quickly and resolutely to stamp out malpractice and even suspended some local authorities altogether. Appointments procedures, auditing and other practices were reformed and public confidence in local government restored.

The management system was a response to public dissatisfaction with the role of the commissioners who had replaced suspended local authorities. It was first tried in the cities of Cork, Dublin and Limerick and by 1942 was in place throughout Ireland. The Managers themselves have become accepted as being above partisan suspicion. Their role in decision-making had removed political responsibility for controversial decisions from councillors in many instances. In addition, with only infrequent exceptions, local councils have welcomed the initiatives taken by Managers. The Managers, while asserting their independent functions, defer to the democratic legitimacy of the elected representatives. They are also the only senior public servants in the Republic who account for their actions in public, on a monthly basis. However, like other top bureaucrats, their tenure is limited to a seven-year term. The Local Appointments Commission (LAC) selects Managers, which has been a major factor in establishing the reputation for honesty and diligence of local government officers.

In the 1960s, Seán Lemass recognised that local authorities had an expanded role to play in national development. He talked of local authorities as 'development corporations' and most Managers have sought to fulfil this role, despite legal and financial restrictions. The Managers have offered leadership in policy formulation and direction generally. Traditionally, the contribution of elected politicians has been to legitimise the leadership offered by their Manager and to ease the execution of policy by intervening on behalf of aggrieved citizens. In future, they may take a more proactive role, but they will still experience electoral pressure to adopt a very local perspective.

Some controversial powers of local government

The only major exceptions to the established understanding between politicians and the City or County Manager arise in relation to planning controls. Councillors in some authorities make regular use of their residual power to overturn a Manager's decision as it applies to a particular individual. This power is generally described with reference to its statutory basis in Section 4 of the County Management Act 1955. A Section 4 motion, if passed, permits a council to direct the Manager to act in a specific instance in a particular way. Typically, it allows planning permission to an individual where general criteria would indicate refusal. Often such cases concern the building of individual houses outside the general terms of the development plan for the area.

The other major display of 'councillor power' comes with the adoption and adaptation of the local development plan. Each major council is the planning authority for its area and as such is legally obliged to draw up a development plan showing the proposed pattern of land use. Thus, the development plan divides the county or city into zones in which residential, agricultural, industrial or other activities will predominate. Planning applications are allowed or refused with reference to the development plan. Clearly, the commercial value of land is markedly influenced by the category into which it is zoned. The pressure on politicians to assert their legal rights can be very great and developers often offer to provide extra amenities, such as sports facilities and parks, if land is made available for residential or industrial use. As we shall see in Chapter 6, in some instances, notably in Dublin, the inducements offered by developers were of more direct personal or political benefit to councillors.

Controversial in some local authorities has been the approval of the annual budget, with some councillors refusing to adopt the Manager's estimates. The issue, in almost all cases, has been the inclusion of new service charges to which the councillors object. This was particularly disputatious in the Dublin area councils. The Minister for the Environment threatened to remove such authorities from office and to appoint commissioners in their place. On each occasion, however, as with Dublin Corporation in 2001, the councils eventually adopted the estimates after a period of protest and brinkmanship. The real conflict, needless to say, had been between the council and central government rather than with the Manager.

The reform of local government

In March 1991, an expert committee, asked by the government to look into the structures and functions (though not the funding) of local government, recommended fairly radical reforms. Like various reports before it, however, the Barrington Report (as it became known) was followed by minimal changes. Legislation in 1992 provided for a slight relaxation of the *ultra vires* rule, which empowered councils to take actions not formerly permitted which might be 'in the interests of the local community'. It did not, however, include a prohibition on the 'dual mandate' that Barrington had proposed. This would also have prevented TDs, Senators and Members of the European Parliament (MEPs) from being councillors. When this idea reappeared in the Local Government Bill of 2000, it was successfully resisted by TDs.

Another reform contained in the legislative proposals of 2000 was the strengthening of the institution of Lord Mayor, or chair of council. Currently these posts are largely ceremonial and are filled annually by election within the council. A former Lord Mayor of Dublin has suggested having a directly elected mayor standing on a city-wide basis – as in some US cities. Such a democratically responsible official could more easily resist the pressures of local councillors; the new Mayor or chairperson would complement the leadership role of the Manager and help in the formulation and accomplishment of difficult policies. Incumbent councillors, however, see the proposal as undermining their position and providing political opportunities for potential rivals. The change has been successfully vetoed by local political pressure. In the local elections of 1999, a gratuity scheme facilitated the retirement of longstanding councillors. There has also been an expansion in the use of committees, including strategic policy committees (SPCs), aimed at enhancing the policy role of members and involving more citizen participation.

Many see the crucial weakness of local government in the Republic as its lack of a significant element of local taxation. Charging for local services is highly controversial and, therefore, limited. To address the lack of local government financial stability, the Local Government Act 1998 established a local government fund financed from an exchequer contribution and the proceeds of motor taxation. The fund is allocated to local authorities as a general fund, to be spent at their discretion.

There was no recognition of local government in Bunreacht na hÉireann until recently. The Constitution Review Group recommended that a form of 'recognition in principle of local government' should be inserted in the Constitution, as in most other EU states. It would also be in accordance with the European Charter of Local Self-Government of the Council of Europe, which the government adopted in 1998. The Taoiseach, Bertie Ahern, gave a political commitment in November 1998 that, at the next available opportunity, there would be a constitutional amendment recognising local government. The amendment was passed by referendum in June 1999. The amendment also set a maximum of five years between local elections.

Regions

The attitude of central government to local government is heavily influenced by the belief that Ireland already has too many elected local authorities and members. Eight regional authorities were nevertheless established in 1994. They are statutory bodies comprising local elected representatives, selected by constituent local authorities. In total, the regional authorities have 220 members. Their main tasks are to promote the coordination of public services in their regions and to review and advise on the implementation of EU Structural and Cohesion Fund Programmes.

State-sponsored industries

A main plank in the agenda of the nationalist movement in Ireland was to control market conditions and build up Irish industry. As we have seen, this was Fianna Fáil's main economic strategy. Thus, when it took office in 1932, tariffs were placed on imports to encourage Irish entrepreneurs to set up manufacturing businesses. This policy certainly helped to widen the Irish manufacturing base by protecting it from outside competition. Reliance on the domestic market, however, kept industrial concerns relatively small, and uncompetitive in international markets. Moreover, there were also essential economic and service functions which did not attract private investment. In these cases successive governments, none of which had any particular ideological preference for state industry, did not hesitate to establish semi-autonomous state-sponsored bodies to perform them.

The commercial state-sponsored bodies operate like private companies in that they are expected to make profits to cover their operations and expansion. There are other non-commercial bodies involved in regulating aspects of Irish life, such as nursing, or advising on policies. The best known of the advisory bodies is the NESC, which brings together representatives of the major economic interests to discuss policy. The NESC's chairperson is the Secretary General of the Department of An Taoiseach; its influence is, therefore, quite direct. It is the commercial bodies, however, that are most controversial. Many are major economic actors, such as the Electricity Supply Board and Aer Lingus, the state-owned national airline. They often enjoyed significant monopoly power and have been the focus of pressure for more liberal market regimes. EU anti-monopoly and free competition legislation has presented them with particular challenges. Competition from the private sector has, for example, become very evident for Aer Lingus, with the privately owned Ryanair now operating a range of services to and from Ireland, Britain and other parts of Europe.

Many state-sponsored bodies have been restructured with the loss of thousands of workers to prepare them either for sharper competitive conditions or sale to private owners. The telecommunications sector is a particularly controversial example. In line with EU policy, the market was liberalised in the late 1990s. The state monopoly provider, Telecom Éireann, was sold in a flotation aimed at small investors. Many thousands of people bought shares for the first time. Their holdings, however, quickly fell in value. The new company, Eircom, operates in a global business world and, through its commercial dealings, the control of telecommunications in Ireland and the profits from them now rest abroad. Many predict a similar pattern for air transport once Aer Lingus is privatised.

Be that as it may, the 100 or so state-sponsored bodies still employ almost 75,000 people, about a third of the public service. The heads of these larger semi-state or state-sponsored bodies have a clear and direct role in public policy. They have open communications with ministers and senior civil servants in their 'parent' departments. As commercial enterprises, they also invest large sums of money in important infrastructural projects and the government takes a close interest in all their plans. Indeed, the government itself appoints the directors and board or council members who make up the management bodies of state-sponsored companies.

The political importance of some of these companies arises from their dependence on public funding; the significance of others, especially those promoting economic development, comes from their influence on the key function of job creation. After a 1994 rationalisation of industrial promotion activities, several bodies now share this responsibility: Bord Fáilte is the Irish Tourist Board; Enterprise Ireland has responsibility for encouraging indigenous industry; the IDA is charged with attracting investment from abroad; the Shannon Free Airport Development Company and Udarás na Gaeltachta (an authority for development in the Irish-speaking regions) promote investment in their own particular areas; and Forfás (the policy and advisory board for industrial development) has a coordinating role among these and other agencies with employment-generation roles. To an extent, all these compete with one other to develop plans, secure investment and influence government policy.

Legislators and policy-making

The role of legislators in the policy process in parliamentary systems is in practice rather restricted. Ireland is certainly no exception. The executive branch, the government, controls the Dáil by party discipline, by the generation of legislation, by the allocation of parliamentary time and, not least, by the control of information. Only at times of intense public excitement, such as the fall of the Reynolds-led government in 1994, is the Dáil central to policy-making. In such periods, the televised debates of Dáil proceedings become the focus of public interest. Generally, however, the main action is taking place elsewhere.

To redress the imbalance of power between the executive and the legislature somewhat, the Oireachtas has sought to strengthen its committee system. A fillip to this project came from the inadequacy of accountability highlighted by alleged financial scandals involving the state-sponsored bodies in 1991 and the beef industry in 1992. Clearly, Dáil methods for obtaining information from ministers or civil servants were hopelessly inadequate. In 1993, therefore, the Dáil committee system was overhauled and new standing committees established. These bodies are better resourced than those that preceded them and the backbench TD in the chair is paid for his or her pains. The committees can summon senior public servants to give evidence, though there was initially some resistance by civil servants when called. As a result, legislation has widened the powers of the Dáil committees to compel witnesses to attend.

This power and its augmented resources permitted the PAC in 2000 to uncover major banking irregularities, which led to substantial payments being made in tax settlements (see Chapter 6). This success greatly enhanced the prestige of the PAC and committees generally.

Ministers must also discuss their plans with legislative committees and the committees themselves can initiate legislation. The Dáil may thus be able to increase its role in the policy process in the future. In December 2000, the government announced plans to change the *modus operandi* of the Dáil, but several important barriers remain. TDs and Senators may find that the burdens of constituency business, local authority membership and party duties leave insufficient time for the committee work. The government is likely to be more parsimonious with support services than TDs would wish. Further, though parliamentarians enjoy privilege against libel for what they say, witnesses and the reporting media do not. As a result, the committee process may be inhibited somewhat. Finally, the government parties have retained a majority on each of the twenty-one committees as well as holding the chair of most of them. It may not, therefore, be in the committees' interests to be too disruptive.

The office of the Ombudsman augments the investigative powers of the Dáil. The Ombudsman has the power to investigate the actions of government departments, local authorities and the postal and telecommunications services. Besides annual reports to the Dáil, the Ombudsman is free to make special reports at any time. However, these reports address individual complaints of poor public service rather than broad policy – because the Ombudsman's role is limited to monitoring and promoting administrative accountability. In 1996, the Constitution Review Group called for the Ombudsman's office to be strengthened, possibly by means of a new article in the Constitution. Meanwhile, new legislation on freedom of information and the Ombudsman's regulatory powers have brought the office in from the margins of the policy process (see also Chapter 6).

Conclusion

In this chapter, we have seen that public policy is constrained by private interests and commercial realities, which are largely shaped by Ireland's place in the world economic order. Demographic, climatic and environmental factors also have a role in determining what governments do. Within these constraints, and despite the increasing importance of the EU in policy-making, Ireland does have important decisions to make. To the extent that the political system has autonomy, powerful figures in public life can make a significant impact, given the political and economic opportunity. However, much too much emphasis is placed on the explanatory value of the activity of 'great men'.

Local government in Ireland, as an independent, adequately resourced and innovative part of the nation's life, has been on the decline since the 1970s.

The keys to its reduced role are the lack of sufficient truly local revenue, the neglect of its long-term future by central government and some public indifference to local democracy.

The making of Irish public policy is dominated by a relatively small number of politicians and high-level public servants. The process is often an incremental and annual one, though there have been some radical turning points. Economic policy, taxation and government expenditure are central to the concerns of all recent Irish governments. On these issues, there is a remarkably broad consensus among the politicians and in the public service. On most policies, therefore, the bureaucrats are very influential. Politicians ultimately take public responsibility and their attention to policy is greatest when either controversy or specific political commitments are high.

Notes

1   C. H. Murray, 'A working and changeable instrument', *Administration*, Vol. 30, No. 4, 1982, p. 44.
2   *Ibid.*

Further reading

Coakley, J. and Gallagher, M. (eds), *Politics in the Republic of Ireland*, 2nd edition, Dublin: Folens, 1993.

Collins, N., *Local Government Managers at Work*, Dublin: Institution of Public Administration, 1987.

Collins, N. (ed.), *Political Issues in Ireland Today*, 2nd edition, Manchester: Manchester University Press, 1999.

Dooney, S. and O'Toole, J., *Irish Government Today*, Dublin: Gill & Macmillan, 1991.

Lee, J., *Ireland 1912–1985: Politics and Society*, Cambridge: Cambridge University Press, 1989.

Government of Ireland, *Devolution Commission – Interim Report*, Dublin: Stationery Office, 1996.

Knox, C. and Haslam, R., 'Local and regional reforms', in N. Collins, (ed.), *Political Issues in Ireland Today*, 2nd edition, Manchester: Manchester University Press, 1999.

5

The Constitution and the law

As we have already noted in Chapter 1, the present Constitution, Bunreacht na hÉireann, came into operation on 29 December 1937. Since then there have been several important constitutional changes, arising both from amendments and from judicial interpretation. Moreover, in recent years the Constitution has become more than ever a focus for the attention of political parties and pressure groups. In 1995 a Constitution Review Group, chaired by former senior civil servant T. K. Whitaker, was set up to determine whether modifications were needed and what these might be. Its report was published in July 1996, but it has as yet had little effect. This chapter looks at the provisions of the Constitution, at its origins and at the wider system of law within which it is located.

What is a Constitution?

The principles of liberal democracy were fashioned and tested in the French and American revolutions at the end of the eighteenth century. The rule of law and the pivotal position of the Constitution are of utmost importance to a democratic system of government. Liberal democratic theory essentially grew up in reaction to the rule of the many by the few. At its base was the notion of 'individual liberty'. For liberal democratic theorists, the power of government comes from the people; governments ought therefore to represent the will of the people, by mechanisms such as consultation, election and plebiscites or referendums. It was also recognised that if the tyranny of a minority could exist, so too could the tyranny of the majority. The freedom of the individual had to be guaranteed, therefore; and an agreed set of rules and standards, to be used as an objective test of the protection given to individuals against the government, was established under the concept of 'the rule of law'. The essential basis of this law was the Constitution; and, allowing for the notable exception of Britain, this was expected to be a written document, endorsed either directly or indirectly by the people over whom it held sway.

What is a Constitution for?

A Constitution does several things:

- It outlines the structure of government. The liberal democratic form of government is distinguished by the separation of the powers given to the legislature, the executive and the judiciary.
- It reflects and codifies the values and beliefs of society, often with an accompanying Bill of Rights.
- It is frequently a statement of intent – it presents an image of what the people would like their society to be. This is particularly the case in countries experiencing great social or political upheaval.

Because a Constitution is the supreme source of law, it is usually made more difficult to change than other laws. Often the wording can be altered only when the people have been consulted in a referendum. A Constitution usually also provides for judicial review. Thus, although judges cannot change the words, the meaning of words, or the meaning of phrases, they can in effect create new rights and obligations. Moreover, this process can sometimes produce an interpretation of the Constitution which is quite contrary to what was previously believed to be the case. This aspect of constitutional change will be looked at more closely below.

Newly independent countries frequently experience an initial period of relatively rapid constitutional change. This was the case with Ireland, which has had three Constitutions: one in 1919, another in 1922 and the present one in 1937. A further change of some constitutional importance was brought about by the 1948 Republic of Ireland Act, which, as the name suggests, made formal the status of the state a republic.

The first and second Constitutions

It is noteworthy that while the leaders of the Irish independence struggle were attempting to throw off British rule, their 1919 Constitution accepted the Westminster parliamentary system as a model for the new Irish government. Although the members of Sinn Féin asserted in principle and in practice their right to armed struggle, they were also strongly schooled in, and accepted the ideals of, constitutional politics. The Constitution of 1919 reflected the predominantly liberal democratic nature of the independence movement, as well as the influence of Sinn Féin's legal advisers, who were mostly trained in the British legal system.

The second Constitution, which was called the 'Constitution of the Irish Free State', also broadly followed the British model. It set up a two-chamber or bicameral parliament (Oireachtas), consisting of a lower house (Dáil) and an upper house (Seanad), with a Cabinet government responsible to the Dáil. The Seanad consisted of members elected by a restricted franchise and others appointed by the head of the government. There were, however, some differences from constitutional practice in Britain, including some measures to make the government more responsible to the people:

- full adult suffrage, covering both men and women, was introduced (six years before Britain did so);
- election by proportional representation was prescribed – so as to ensure representation of minorities;
- there were provisions for the initiation of legislation from outside the Oireachtas and for the calling of referendums to test public opinion on legislation;
- and, following the example of France and the United States, the Constitution of the Irish Free State also included a declaration of rights – including freedom of expression, religion and association, the principle of habeas corpus and the inviolability of the citizen's home.

When Fianna Fáil was elected to government in 1932, it was plain that the Constitution would come under critical review, if only because it was based on the Anglo-Irish Treaty. De Valera's primary intention was to remove all vestiges of British control in Ireland from the Constitution. The years between 1933 and 1937 were used to get rid of what Fianna Fáil considered to be the most objectionable parts of the 1922 governmental arrangements. The links with Britain were lessened by the removal of the oath to the Crown and the virtual abolition of the office of Governor-General (the monarch's representative in the Free State). In 1936, de Valera took advantage of the abdication of King Edward VIII to remove any role for the British Crown from the Constitution also. And finally, in 1937, he moved to introduce the new Bunreacht na hÉireann, the third Irish Constitution.

The tone of the 1937 Constitution

This Constitution plainly mirrored de Valera's views and represented a further break with Britain. The system of government specified was in the mould of that in numerous other liberal democratic states: sovereignty lay with the people; the head of state, the President, was to be elected; Parliament was to consist of two houses; there would be a separate and independent judiciary. In addition, like some other written constitutions, Bunreacht na hÉireann contained an inventory of positive social principles; and it guaranteed certain individual rights. An obviously Roman Catholic ethos pervaded these provisions.

In the articles on the family and its protection – especially the ban on divorce and the prescriptive attitude to the role of women as homemakers – the Constitution clearly reflected Catholic teaching of the 1930s.

The President

As head of state, the President performs a range of formal acts of government as well as being the symbol of the state in ceremonial functions both at home and abroad. The Irish President is not the head of government, as in the United States or France – the head of government in Ireland is the Taoiseach. Nor is the Irish President the source of governmental power, as is the British monarchy. De Valera claimed the President 'is there to guard the people's rights and mainly to guard the Constitution'. The President's role as representative of the people is signified by the provision that he or she be directly elected every seven years; and the President may be re-elected once only. On four occasions the main political parties have agreed on one candidate and no election was necessary. Thus, for example, President Patrick Hillery renominated himself at the expiry of his first term of seven years in 1983 and was not opposed.

The last presidential election was held in November 1997. The then sitting President, the first woman to hold the office, did not run for a second term. An internationally known figure, Mary Robinson decided instead to accept an appointment as United Nations Human Rights Commissioner. After a hard-fought election between candidates of the three main parties and two independents, she was succeeded by Mary McAleese, a senior university academic from Belfast nominated by Fianna Fáil and the first person from Northern Ireland to become President.

The powers of the President

- The President may refer any bill to the Supreme Court to test whether it is constitutional. If a government wishes to proceed with a bill declared repugnant to the Constitution, it must submit it to a referendum.
- A majority of the Seanad together with not less than one-third of TDs may ask the President not to sign a bill, because it is of such importance that the people should be consulted. It will then be signed only if approved by referendum, or by a new Dáil elected after a dissolution.
- The President may convene a meeting of the houses of the Oireachtas; this is intended to cover an emergency where those whose job it is to call a meeting cannot, or will not.
- The Dáil is summoned and dissolved by the President, on the advice of the Taoiseach. If the Taoiseach has lost the support of the majority of TDs, the President may refuse a dissolution, giving the Dáil a chance to elect a different Taoiseach and avoid a general election.

- If the Dáil and government wish to restrict the time a bill may be considered by the Seanad, the President must concur.
- The President may rule in a dispute between the Ceann Comhairle (the 'Speaker' of the Dáil) and the Seanad about whether a bill is a 'money bill', that is one in which the Seanad's role is very restricted.

As will be clear, there is little scope for the President to exercise other than negative power. The office has remained largely ceremonial and above controversy, and keeping the head of state above party politics or public contention was a priority for the Constitution Review Group (see above). Its report made in 1996 called for little change in the powers and functions of the President. The only exception was that the President's power to refuse a dissolution of the Dáil should be replaced with a measure to allow a 'constructive vote of no confidence' by the Dáil. The intention was that the Dáil would nominate an alternative Taoiseach and the President would not become embroiled in party political issues. As with so many of the Group's recommendations, nothing has yet been done to implement this.

On one occasion, in 1976, the President actually resigned in order to ensure that the office did not become associated with political controversy. President Cearbhall O'Dálaigh, acting entirely properly in terms of the responsibilities of his office, referred the Emergency Powers Bill of the then Fine Gael/Labour government to the Supreme Court for a decision on its constitutionality. The Bill arose directly from the troubles in Northern Ireland and from the effects these were having in the Republic. Although the Bill could not be declared unconstitutional because the government had proclaimed a state of emergency, the President believed that the Court had the power nevertheless to enquire into the existence of a genuine state of emergency.

Some government members were privately critical of this action, but there was little public concern about the matter. However, the Minister for Defence, Patrick Donegan, claimed that the President was a 'thundering disgrace' because of his actions. President O'Dálaigh thought this 'outrageous criticism' had brought his office into disrepute and the refusal of the Taoiseach to accept Donegan's resignation made it seem that he was standing by his Minister's remarks. So the President resigned. Clearly, he had been put in an impossible position by the government's response. Moreover, the offence was compounded because the Minister's remarks were made at an army function and supreme command of the defence forces is vested in the President.

President Robinson was a constitutional lawyer and generally sought to enhance the role of head of state. Not surprisingly, therefore, she exercised her powers more often than any of her predecessors. Of the nine bills which were referred to the Supreme Court in the first six years of her presidency, four were found – at least in part – to be repugnant to the Constitution. President Robinson also addressed both houses of the Oireachtas in joint session more often than any previous holder of the office. President McAleese is also a lawyer (having held for a time the same Chair in Law at Trinity College, Dublin, which Mary Robinson once occupied) and she too seems intent on exploring and enhancing the role of President. A devout Catholic, she is an equally devout ecumenist and caused the Roman Catholic Archbishop of Dublin implicitly to criticise her for her full participation in a Church of Ireland communion service.

The Seanad

The upper house, Seanad Éireann, has sixty members. It has a subordinate position in the Oireachtas. The Seanad's membership was originally intended to reflect the principle of 'vocationalism' (see Table 5.1). It should be noted that the idea that major interest groups as well as ordinary voters ought to have parliamentary representation held great sway in Catholic and conservative movements in the 1930s.

Despite the ostensible vocationalism of the Seanad, in reality it soon became dominated as much by party politics as the lower house. This is hardly surprising, since the Taoiseach nominates eleven Senators, while the electorate for the forty-three vocational members is made up of people already holding elected office themselves – members of the Oireachtas as well as all county and county borough councillors. The final six Senators are elected (three each) by the graduates, first, of Trinity College (University of Dublin) and, second, of the constituent colleges of the National University of Ireland (Dublin, Cork, Galway and Maynooth). Within the enabling provisions of the Seventh Amendment of the Constitution, however, the arrangements for the election of these Senators may be revised. Although no action has yet been taken on this, it must be a possibility since there are two newer universities – the University of Limerick and Dublin City University – which are not represented. There is, on the other hand, a widespread view – shared by the Constitution Review Group – that this essentially elitist provision which gives university graduates alone an additional vote should be done away with altogether.

Table 5.1. *Vocational panels for Seanad elections*

Panel	Seats
Agriculture	11
Culture and Education	5
Industry and Commerce	9
Labour	11
Public Administration	7

De Valera felt the real value of the Seanad lay in checking, redrafting and amending legislation. So the Seanad's powers are limited to revising and clarifying bills, together with some minor constitutional duties and rights. Compared with the House of Lords, the second chamber of the British Parliament, the Seanad has no power of substance and this is especially so in relation to financial matters. However, it does perform other useful political functions. The Seanad is often used as a slow route out of politics for retiring TDs, or as a temporary political home for those who have failed to get re-elected. It has also been useful way for would-be TDs to make an initial entry on to the parliamentary scene. It is worthy of mention that the Constitution Review Group has suggested that consideration be given to abolishing the Seanad.

The Dáil and the government

According to the Constitution, the government will consist of not less than seven and not more than fifteen members. The Taoiseach, the Tánaiste (Deputy Prime Minister) and the Minister for Finance must be members of the Dáil. All other members of the government must be members of the Oireachtas, though only two of them can come from the Seanad. In practice, very few ministers have ever been appointed from the Seanad. Ministers have the right to attend and to speak in either house, but the government is respon-sible to the Dáil alone.

The lower house of the Oireachtas, Dáil Éireann, has varied in size from 128 seats to 166 at present. (There has to be one TD for every 20,000 to 30,000 electors.) The country is at present divided into forty-one constitu-encies and their boundaries must be revised at least once every twelve years to take account of population changes. The Dáil lasts for a maximum of five years. A general election must take place not later than thirty days after the dissolution and the newly elected Dáil must meet within thirty days of the polling date.

Ministers of government

Each member of the government usually becomes the minister (or head) of one department of state – and occasionally of two. Apart from the members of government there can also be up to seventeen Ministers of State, or junior ministers, who help their seniors in parliamentary and departmental duties. One Minister of State in the Department of An Taoiseach with special re-sponsibilities is the government chief whip – who is the main information conduit between government and backbench TDs and who attends govern-ment meetings as of right. In the Fine Gael/Labour/DL government formed in December 1994, it was agreed that an additional Minister of State would have

a right to attend Cabinet meetings. This practice continued in the Fianna Fáil/
PD coalition, whereby a junior minister from the minority party is entitled to
be present at Cabinet. Also, other Ministers of State are occasionally invited
to attend if an item within their particular area of responsibility is up for
discussion or decision.

The government has exclusive initiative in matters of finance. Article 17
of the Constitution states:

> Dáil Éireann may not pass any vote or resolution and no law shall be enacted
> for the appropriation of revenue or other public moneys, unless the purpose of
> the appropriation shall have been recommended to Dáil Éireann by a message
> from the Government signed by the Taoiseach.

As noted above, the power the Seanad has over finances is highly limited: it
may make recommendations but not substantive changes.

Amendments to the Constitution

From 1941 until 1972, Bunreacht na hÉireann remained unchanged. After
an initial transitional period during which amendment was easier than it was
later to be, Ireland's Constitution was essentially settled for over thirty years.
It can be changed only by referendum, of which there have been several in
recent years. In total since 1937 there have been eighteen amendments –
including two passed before the end of the transition period in June 1941,
which did not require popular approval (see Table 5.2).

Judicial review

The provision for judicial review in Bunreacht na hÉireann can be found at
three points: Article 15.4.1 forbids the Oireachtas to pass any law repugnant
to the Constitution; Article 34.3.2 gives the power of review to the High
Court; and Article 34.4.3 allows the High Court's decisions on such questions
to be appealed to the Supreme Court. The powers of the courts are, in this
respect, greater than in some other liberal democracies; in particular, they
can pronounce on the constitutionality of legislation both before and after it
is passed. In the United States, by contrast, the courts can rule on a piece of
law only *after* it has gone through the full legislative process. In France, courts
can rule on proposals only *before* they become law. In the UK, broadly speaking, no review of constitutionality is permitted – even though this seems to
be challenged by EU membership.

It is only relatively recently, however, that the provisions of Bunreacht na
hÉireann have been changed through judicial *interpretation* – rather than by

Table 5.2. *Constitutional referendums since 1937*

Year	Subject
1937	Plebiscite to adopt the Constitution
1959*	Introducing a new non-PR voting system
1968*	Reducing the size of Dáil constituencies
1968*	Introducing a new non-PR voting system
1972	Approving EU membership
1972	Lowering the voting age from twenty-one to eighteen
1972	Removing the 'special position' of the Roman Catholic Church
1979	Clarifying child adoption procedures
1979	Extending the graduate electorate for the Seanad
1983	Protecting the unborn – prohibition of abortion
1984	Extending voting rights to certain non-citizens
1986*	Removing the prohibition on divorce
1987	Approving the Single European Act
1992	Approving the Maastricht Treaty
1992*	Restricting the availability of abortion
1992	Guaranteeing a right to travel for abortion
1992	Guaranteeing a right to information on abortion
1995	Removing the prohibition on divorce
1997	Reaffirming Cabinet confidentiality
1998	Amendments to Articles 2 and 3, consequent on the Belfast 'Good Friday' Agreement
1998	Approving the Amsterdam Treaty
1999	Recognition of local government and the timing of local elections

*In these cases the proposition was defeated.

changes in its wording by means of referendums. From the 1960s onwards there was a growing realisation by Irish jurists that the Constitution provided 'hidden' legal guarantees as regards the fundamental rights of individuals. There are several reasons why such possibilities were not fully realised before then and further reasons why the situation changed when it did.

First, until the mid-1960s, Irish lawyers were generally schooled in the British common law tradition. Britain does not have a written Constitution and, in the absence of a Bill of Rights or its equivalent, relies on common law, or precedent, for the protection of the individual: against an attack upon his or her person; against the abuse of power by those set in authority; in defence of free speech, and so on. There are, therefore, no defined reference points as regards the maintenance of social justice; and the sovereignty of Parliament in the making of laws is considered absolute.

Second, the early years of Bunreacht na hÉireann were dominated by the war in Europe and by internal subversion then and later, such as the IRA's cross-border bombing and shooting campaign of the late 1950s. These were periods of increased security legislation (during the Second World War, a state of emergency was declared and a standing military court set up). An atmosphere thus existed which militated against the development of constitutional provision on citizens' rights.

That position changed in the 1960s. The security situation improved and emergency legislation was no longer required (although it remained on the statute book). More positively, Ireland's economic prosperity increased significantly and higher living standards helped stem the flow of emigration. Consequently, the population became both younger and increasingly influenced by more cosmopolitan ideas. Further, there was change within the legal profession itself: standards of legal education improved; many students went to law schools in the United States and recognised the constitutional parallels with Ireland; new people began to dominate in the court structure; and by the early 1970s there was a majority of 'progressive' or 'liberal' judges in the Supreme Court. They became increasingly willing to reinterpret the Constitution and more groups sought to pursue or protect their interests in this way.

The consequences

The main result of increasing judicial reinterpretation has been the augmentation of individual rights (see Table 5.3). Articles 40 to 44 of the Constitution list fundamental rights which 'the State guarantees in its laws to respect and, as far as practicable ... to defend and vindicate' (Article 40.3.1). However, it was decided by Justice Kenny in 1965 that the personal rights that may be invoked to invalidate legislation are not confined to those specified in Article 40. They also include all those rights which 'result from the Christian and democratic nature of the State'. Since this ruling, several rights unspecified in the Constitution have been recognised and enforced (see Table 5.3).

The Constitution has thus been developed by the 'implication' of rights – especially by reference to sections of it previously 'unused' – as well as by interpretation. Thus, for instance, the Preamble to Bunreacht na hÉireann was generally thought to be of little significance. It notes, *inter alia*, that the people are:

> seeking to promote the common good, with due observance of Prudence, Justice and Charity, so that the dignity and freedom of the individual may be assured, true social order attained, the unity of our country restored, and concord established with other nations.

This has been taken up by the judiciary for the purpose of keeping the Constitution and the law flowing from it in touch with prevailing ideas. Critics, on the other hand, maintain that in doing this the judges are stepping over the boundary between the law and politics and in particular are breaching the understanding that, in liberal democracies, laws should be made only by

Table 5.3. *Citizens' rights in Ireland*

Specified in Bunreacht na hÉireann	Ruled by judicial interpretation to be implied
Equality before the law	To bodily integrity
Personal liberty	To marital privacy
Privacy of the dwelling of every citizen	To privacy of communication
To express convictions and opinions freely	To dispose of and withdraw one's labour
To assemble peaceably and without arms	Not to belong to a trade union
To form associations and unions	To earn one's livelihood
To family, education, private property	To work
Freedom of religion	To litigate claims
	To prepare for and follow a chosen career
	To consult with, and be represented by, a lawyer when charged with a serious criminal offence
	To be assisted by the state if one's health is in jeopardy
	To marry
	To free movement within the state

Based on: A. J. Foley and S. Lalor (eds), *Annotated Constitution of Ireland 1937–1994*, Dublin: Gill & Macmillan, 1995, *passim*.

Parliament. Nevertheless, individuals and groups seeking to restrain government action have won several judgements by the Supreme Court. Thus, for example, a member of the European Parliament, Patricia McKenna, succeeded in having the Supreme Court declare unconstitutional the use of public money by the government to fund its pro-divorce campaign before the 1995 referendum (see below).

However, slightly out of the general run, the government itself took an action of the same kind somewhat earlier to have reaffirmed a constitutional requirement that had effectively fallen into disuse. In 1992 the Attorney-General (the government's chief legal adviser) applied for and got a total ban on the disclosure of discussions which had taken place at any Cabinet meeting in the past – on the grounds that the Constitution called for complete secrecy, even though Cabinet proceedings had been the subject of informal press briefings for many years. Thus, words written in the 1930s which codified contemporary convention were used to reverse the more flexible practices of the 1990s.

Portentously perhaps, it is to the Preamble and Articles 40 to 44 that the 1996 Constitution Review Group suggested the most radical rewording – to allow for *de facto* changes in society since the 1930s.

Ireland and European law

Ireland is a sovereign, independent, democratic State.
(Bunreacht na hÉireann, Article 5)

Another significant influence on the development of the Irish legal system has been the EU. As a product of Ireland's historical experience, the Constitution emphasises the notion of *national* sovereignty. An amendment to the Constitution was thus necessary to enable the Republic to become a full member of the EU, since membership involved some surrender of Irish sovereignty. This first 'European' amendment was approved by a large majority and has been followed by three more. In December 1985 the then European Community adopted the Single European Act (SEA), intended to speed up and make more democratic its decision-making process; to be implemented, it had to be ratified by each national Parliament. In Ireland, however, there was a successful court challenge to the SEA, on the grounds that it was unconstitutional. In particular, the Supreme Court ruled that Title III of the SEA represented a pooling or transferring of sovereignty and thus exceeded the normal and necessary constitutional power of an Irish government to conclude international agreements. The outcome was a second 'European' amendment, passed in 1987, which allowed Ireland to ratify the SEA. The third was passed in 1992, permitting ratification of the EU's Maastricht Treaty. Another, in 1998, sanctioned the provisions of the Treaty of Amsterdam.

Article 15.2.1 of the Constitution states that 'The sole and exclusive power of making laws for the State is hereby vested in the Oireachtas; no other legislative authority has power to make laws for the State'. Despite that, European Community law applies directly in member states, to governments, companies and individuals. Its obligations, or the rights it establishes, must be upheld by national courts and then by the European Court of Justice. The EU, in effect, makes laws for Irish citizens, although they have not been passed by the Oireachtas. Irish ministers and MEPs are, of course, involved in the process of lawmaking at the EU level.

There are five ways in which EU law can change or otherwise influence Irish law. The Council of Ministers and/or the European Commission can issue regulations, directives, decisions, recommendations and opinions. Regulations have direct effect in Ireland and require little or no domestic action. Directives are binding and may require: a change in administrative practice; secondary legislation – in the form of ministerial orders called 'statutory instruments'; or amended or new legislation. Decisions from the Council and Commission are directly applicable and binding on the government, company or individual to whom they are addressed. The rest – recommendations and opinions – are not legally binding, although they may be considered politically so.

Irish courts are not allowed to review EU statutes, or their compatibility with the Constitution. Much domestic legislation is now a result of obligations placed on Ireland to conform to EU directives. But, until recently at any rate, the parliamentary supervision of EU law has been generally unsatisfactory and debate on EU lawmaking has tended to be perfunctory. In March 1995 a Joint Committee on European Affairs was set up in the Oireachtas for the purpose of improving democratic accountability on EU matters. This has had some beneficial effects, but many TDs and Senators still find little reward in attending to the detail of European legislation. On the other hand, while Irish governments have generally been ardent Europeans, they have been firm in resisting proposals that would result in legislation inimical to Irish interests.

Council of Europe: the European Court of Human Rights

The Council of Europe is made up of twenty-one West European parliamentary democracies and other states. A further 'external' influence on the development of Ireland's legal system has been the Council's European Convention on Human Rights. An aggrieved citizen of a subscribing state, who has exhausted all domestic remedies, may petition the European Court of Human Rights[1] for a ruling that his or her state has violated the rights guaranteed in the Convention on Human Rights.[2] All EU members recognise the jurisdiction of the Court in Strasbourg in human rights cases.

The first major and direct influence of the European Court of Human Rights on the Irish system of justice was to establish that a petitioner must be free – in every sense – to seek redress before national courts. In the case in point, the Court ruled that the expense of legal proceedings had put them outside the reach of the individual concerned. The result was that a form of legal aid provision in civil cases has had to be introduced in the Republic.

As we have already noted, a Constitution is supposed to reflect and codify the values and beliefs of its society. Social values in Ireland, north and south, have generally been more conservative than elsewhere in Europe – especially as regards sexual behaviour. Partly as a consequence, in matters of individual rights, the law and Constitution remained less 'liberal' in Ireland for longer. Indeed, as many defenders of traditional values feared, the European Court has had a substantial impact in this respect. The first important decision arose from a case brought by a private citizen, Geoffrey Dudgeon, before the Northern Ireland courts in 1981, following a European judgement that homosexual activity between consenting adults should be permitted. Although the case was lost on a technicality, it was clear that the European Court ruling meant that the then legislation outlawing such behaviour – not only in Northern Ireland, but also in the Republic – violated a guaranteed right to privacy under the European Convention on Human Rights.

The case increased the concern of those wishing to retain Ireland's less liberal laws that they might be changed 'from outside'. This anxiety was vividly displayed in the campaign for the Eighth Amendment (see below). In

1988 the European Court again showed its importance for Ireland by upholding the claim of a Trinity College university lecturer and independent member of the Seanad, David Norris, that his rights were infringed by the criminal law on homosexuality. To meet the requirements of the Norris judgement, in 1993 the government introduced new legislation on homosexual behaviour – replacing the then existing British-made laws which dated back to 1861 and 1865.

Ireland signed the European Convention on Human Rights in 1953. It accepted the idea of compulsory implementation, as well as the legislation that followed from Court judgements. The process of obtaining a judgement was, however, long and expensive and this provoked legal commentators to suggest that the Convention ought to be incorporated into domestic law – so that the delay and high cost could be reduced. It was argued, furthermore, that in the climate generated by the troubles in Northern Ireland, the adoption of the Convention in both jurisdictions in Ireland might act as a general reassurance of equality of rights.

However, most politicians were reluctant to face the possibility of an unpredictable and uncontrollable extension of legal support for human rights – testing of the limits of Bunreacht na hÉireann, with the possibility of appeal to the European Court of Human Rights, was regarded as a more than sufficient safeguard. Interestingly, therefore, it was only as a consequence of the Good Friday Agreement in Northern Ireland (see Chapter 7) that the Republic was finally obliged to take the important step of making the European Convention part of the law of the land. The Belfast Agreement also required the Republic to set up its own Human Rights Commission, paralleling and linking with the one north of the border.

The Eighth Amendment

From 1981 until 1983 one of the most divisive debates in the Republic surrounded the eventually successful campaign for the Eighth Amendment to the Constitution to protect the life of the 'unborn'. Abortion seemed to be prohibited perfectly adequately by an 1861 Act. Moreover, the overwhelming majority of those campaigning against the Amendment were at pains to point out that they did *not* want to see abortion introduced; they were against the Eighth Amendment because they saw it as unnecessary and divisive. The campaign can be understood, however, only in terms of a fear that judicial interpretation, whether in Ireland itself or at the European Court of Human Rights, might change the existing law and permit abortion 'by the back door'.

The Eighth Amendment was eventually passed in 1983. It illustrates well the difficulties presented by a written constitution which seeks to make detailed prohibitions and regulations – matters which might better be left to legislation. In due course, the 'X case', as it became known, highlighted ambiguities in the Eighth Amendment. A court injunction was issued under the Amendment in February 1992 restraining a young girl, pregnant as a result of rape, from leaving Ireland to seek an abortion. After numerous twists and turns, including some unexpected judicial rulings, it was necessary to have a triple referendum on various aspects of the abortion issue. Held in November 1992, it showed the public, like its politicians, to be somewhat equivocal. Two proposed amendments, relating to the right to travel (to have an abortion) and the right to information (about the availability of abortion in other countries) were passed; the third, on the more substantive issue of abortion itself, was defeated. The Fianna Fáil/PD government eventually set up an Oireachtas committee to look at the legislative options available to the Dáil in light of both the requirements of the Constitution and the judgement in the X case. At the time of writing its report had not been published, so the questions raised by the X case remained unresolved. While Irish people seem content to permit their fellow citizens to avail of abortion services in another jurisdiction, they are unwilling to permit abortions to be carried out in Ireland.

Divorce and the Constitution

Another constitutional amendment campaign was fought in 1986, this time about the deletion of the article in Bunreacht na hÉireann which decreed that 'no law shall be enacted providing for the grant of a dissolution of marriage' (Article 41.3.2). At the beginning, opinion polls showed a significant majority in favour of the change. However, the public debate became enmeshed in the question of what it seemed might be the inadequate rights of a woman to a share of the family property after a divorce. The opinion polls began a slide which culminated in success for the 'no divorce' side. A case was also taken to the European Court of Human Rights by an Irish couple to test whether the Irish constitutional prohibition on divorce contravened their rights and those of their daughter, but it too was lost.

However, the divorce issue refused to go away. The anti-divorce view remained strong of course, but there were many for whom the availability of divorce was at the very top of what had begun to be called the 'liberal agenda' in Ireland. There were, indeed, people who were personally committed to the Catholic Church's view of lifelong marriage, but for whom the question was nonetheless to do with personal liberty – about freedom of conscience and about the need for Irish society to become more open and pluralistic.

After long and diligent preparation by the government, including legislation in advance to deal with the property rights aspect, in November 1995 the issue of divorce was again put to a referendum. The Irish people are not to be taken for granted, however. For despite the quite remarkable all-party support for the carefully worded proposition, only a slender majority favoured allowing divorce in Ireland. Since then, moreover, the number of divorce cases heard has been a tiny trickle rather than the flood predicted by many observers.

The effects of the 'troubles' in Northern Ireland

For some, the implementation of the liberal agenda, as well as being necessary on its merits, is also important in order to convince Unionists in Northern Ireland that they have nothing to fear from their southern neighbours. However, the major effect of the outbreak of civil unrest in the 1960s was to bring the 'national question' back on to the political stage in the Republic, after a long period of effectively being ignored. Until recently Bunreacht na hÉireann claimed the whole island of Ireland as being 'the national territory' (Article 2). It also asserted that although the Constitution's practical effect was confined to the twenty-six counties, this in no way affected 'the right of the Parliament and Government established by this Constitution to exercise jurisdiction over the whole of [the national] territory' (Article 3).

For Unionists, Articles 2 and 3 came to symbolise what they saw as the hostile territorial ambitions of the Republic. In a case taken by a leading member of the Ulster Unionist Party in 1990 (*McGimpsey* v. *Ireland*), the Supreme Court said that Article 2 was a 'claim of legal right' on the whole island. Further, Article 3 was ruled to be a 'constitutional imperative'. Despite that, the judgement did not specifically oblige the Republic's government to take any action on that score and from 1974 onwards recognition of the status of Northern Ireland as part of the UK was given formal iteration on several occasions. Indeed, at a slightly earlier stage of the Northern Ireland disorder a referendum was held in order to refute, at least to some degree, Unionist assertions that the Republic was a sectarian state. Article 44.1.2 of Bunreacht na hÉireann recognised 'the special position of the Holy Catholic Apostolic and Roman Church as the guardian of the faith professed by the great majority of the citizens'. Cross-party and wide social support ensured the easy passage of a referendum in 1972 calling for its deletion. The Article, it was argued, gave no rights or advantages to the Catholic Church, but it had negative connotations for Protestants and ought thus to be eliminated. Furthermore, as was widely forecast, Articles 2 and 3 were reworded to make them 'aspirational' rather than 'imperative', as part of the new Northern Ireland constitutional settlement in the Belfast 'Good Friday' Agreement (see Chapter 7). These changes, too, gained wide popular citizen support in a subsequent referendum.

Conclusion

Bunreacht na hÉireann retains many of the features of British constitutional practice, to which the authors of Ireland's various Constitutions have looked for a model. It is, however, different in several important respects. The people are sovereign; the head of state is elected; various Catholic sentiments are reflected in its working; vocationalism is the ostensible basis of the second chamber; and, most significant of all, it is written down. In many states the courts, by interpreting the Constitution, play an increasingly forthright role in curbing governments and in effect creating judge-made law. Ireland, while retaining many British constitutional features, therefore, is becoming more like the United States, Germany, South Africa and elsewhere as regards judicial activism. The basis of the authority of judges derives from three sources: the written text; the increased intrusiveness of the state into the citizen's daily life; and broad consent in a popular culture that is cautious about the motives of politicians. In Ireland, the judiciary and jurists have found more scope for activism in the 1937 Constitution than they for long realised. The impact of legislation, especially the increasing number of EU-derived laws, has also alerted Irish citizens to their constitutional rights. Finally, judges still command a high level of public respect for their impartiality and propriety.

Bunreacht na hÉireann is, for all that, still bound by the ideological concerns, the political fears and the political aspirations of its authors. More than sixty years after it was written, some of its provisions appear less well founded than de Valera, its principal progenitor, anticipated. A number of its novel features, such as the vocational second chamber, have developed quite differently than expected. Furthermore, public attitudes today, to matters such as the role of women and relations with Northern Ireland, contrast sharply with those that shaped the original document. Nevertheless, the Constitution as amended, interpreted and informally augmented by politicians, civil servants and judges remains central to Irish politics today. As a working set of rules and principles, it has become the focus of debate about new social and political rights and obligations. Alterations to it are one important measure of the pace of social and political change.

Notes

1 The European Court of Human Rights, based in Strasbourg, should not be confused with the European Court of Justice in Luxembourg, which is the EU's main judicial body.
2 Only a Council of Europe member state's own constitutional provisions cannot be challenged.

Further reading

Chubb, B., *Sourcebook of Irish Government*, Dublin: Institute of Public Administration, 1983.

Doolan, B., *Constitutional Law and Constitutional Rights in Ireland*, Dublin: Gill & Macmillan, 1984.

Farrell, B., *De Valera's Constitution and Ours*, Dublin: Gill & Macmillan, 1988.

Ward, A., *Constitutional Tradition: Government and Modern Ireland, 1782–1992*, Dublin: Irish Academic Press, 1994.

6

Political corruption in Ireland

Neil Collins and Mary O'Shea

The scale and intricacy of political corruption being uncovered by parliamentary and quasi-judicial inquiries has created some turmoil in Irish politics in recent years. There is genuine popular amazement at these phenomena and growing cynicism, which is reflected in a decline in the public standing of politicians. Because corruption appears as a new item on the agenda, it may in fact loom disproportionately large in the minds of Irish commentators. In turn, its level and extent may be misjudged by those from abroad who give intermittent attention to Ireland. To understand corruption in the Republic of Ireland, therefore, it is necessary to examine the concept within an analytical framework that allows for both historical and international comparison. This chapter will also offer some suggestions, derived from the analysis, as to how corruption in Ireland might be reduced or eliminated.

Definitions

Definitions of corruption are broad ranging. Some authors opt for definitions based on laws and other formal rules, because these allow relative precision and stability. Others stress cultural standards so as to accommodate more realistic and subtle definitions. A third school seeks to put the wider political implications of corruption and the moral issues centre-stage. An accepted core element, which is taken here as a working definition, is 'the abuse of public office for private gain'. Such gain is not necessarily financial but is of personal value to those involved.

Corruption is not confined to single transactions. In many circumstances it is part of an ongoing routine by which those with public responsibilities extract personal financial benefit above and beyond their official pay. Corrupt activity is often described using the concept of 'rent seeking', which derives from economics. Rent seeking is a search for opportunities to acquire an extra

Table 6.1. *Types of political corruption*

Incidental	Institutional	Systemic
Small scale	Larger development impact	Huge development impact
Involving individual and very junior public officials such as police officers, customs and and tax officials	Can affect most or all of a government department, or a parastatal organisation such as a procurement agency or marketing board	Wholly corrupt system
Little macro-economic cost, but profound public alienation	Can have a substantial impact upon government revenues and trade diversion	In such circumstances, honesty is 'irrational'
Often hard to curb	Sustained reform effort necessary rather than 'individualised' response	Reform by fundamental change

Source: S. P. Riley, 'The political economy of anti-corruption strategies in Africa', in
M. Robinson (ed.), *Corruption and Development*, London: Frank Cass, 1998.

return which, for public officials or politicians, is over and above their legitimate reward.

The value of the 'rent seeking' concept is the focus it puts on the circumstances that give rise to the *potential* for rent, as well as on institutions or
policies that reduce it. In particular, economists recommend structures that
reduce rent-enhancing elements of discretion in the supply of public services
or elements of monopoly control. We ought, however, to be alert to the limits
of economic models of politics and public management. Patterns of behaviour that may be permissible in the private sector can be outside accepted
norms for those charged with the public interest. Citizens may expect higher
standards than customers, even in the context of public sector reforms that
seek to introduce business practice into the machinery of government. The
economists' certainties are based on the simple assumption that a narrow
understanding of self-interest motivates all actors. It discounts any democratic or public service motive.

Categorisations of corruption are numerous but, following Riley, the three
main forms are incidental (individual), institutional, and systemic or societal
(see Table 6.1). Thus, in some political systems, corruption may involve only
the occasional 'rogue' politician or official and be episodic rather than sustained. In other cases, however, some central or local government departments
or groups of elected officials might be routinely corrupt. Such corruption is

referred to here as 'institutional', but is described by Riley as 'systemic'. It may be associated with one state function, or with a particular ministry or local authority. This institutional corruption may reflect the nature of the task involved, or the laxity of control in terms of, for example, efficient auditing; and such corruption is generally isolated but persistent.

The third category covers the most extreme circumstances. In such systemically corrupt political systems, some form of corruption taints almost every transaction. All state institutions, politicians and, in all likelihood, anyone in social authority will expect to make illicit private gains from official business. Systemic corruption is rare in liberal democracies. When the legitimacy of the government is not in question, when property and contract rights are clear and when the rule of law is broadly upheld, all-pervasive or systemic corruption is difficult to sustain.

Ireland: incidental or institutional corruption?

The question of what type of corruption Ireland may be experiencing is important, since a sustainable strategy for controlling it will depend on properly understanding the problem. The main distinctions made in the literature between incidental and institutional corruption revolve around the following characteristics:

- frequency;
- level;
- controls;
- public trust.

To help us make a judgement in the Irish case, therefore, Table 6.2 sets out how these features differ in both forms of corruption relevant to Irish circumstances.

As always in studies of corruption, the analysis must start by noting that the activity is secretive and covert. It is impossible to know whether the corruption that is exposed is representative or not. An unknowable amount will remain hidden. In Ireland, the legislation used to govern corruption had until recently changed little for almost eighty years. Under the Public Bodies

Table 6.2. *Differing features of forms of corruption*

	Incidental	Institutional
Frequency	Episodic	Routine
Level	One or few persons	Narrow but pervasive
Controls	Generally sufficient	Weak
Public trust	Generally high	Low

Corrupt Practices Act 1889 and the Prevention of Corruption Acts 1906 and 1916, bribery of a public official leaves both giver and receiver open to a seven-year prison sentence.

The Ethics in Public Office Act 1995 updated the law and shifted the burden of proof in some cases. Thus, where senior government or parliamentary office holders are involved, money is deemed to be given corruptly unless proven otherwise. The 1995 Act has made conviction much easier. On the other hand, exposure of corruption through the media is inhibited by relatively high burdens of proof in the law on defamation. The account that follows is clearly assisted by a recent plethora of revelations and inquiries, but it cannot be complete. It concentrates, therefore, on the recent cases, particularly those that are central to recent tribunals and inquiries.

Tribunals and inquiries

The Beef Tribunal

In August 1994, a Tribunal of Inquiry reported on the Irish beef processing industry, which accounted for 34 per cent of Ireland's agricultural output. Serious charges of corruption were made in the Dáil before the setting up of the Tribunal, which was prompted principally by revelations in a British television programme. Established parliamentary methods, however, were unable to elicit the full facts. The report of the Beef Tribunal discovered:

* irregularities in the way employees of processing companies conducted their business;
* inadequate control exercised by government departments;
* poor political judgements in the management of public affairs.

The report raised disturbing questions about the quality of public administration in Ireland, the relationship between business and politics, and the issue of political party funding. The too-easy identification of an area of commonality between state and private interests is a key feature of the case. It is clear that ministers, and to some extent civil servants, regarded the success of certain beef enterprises as being essential to the wider national interest.

The McCracken Tribunal

This was set up in early 1997 to examine the relationships of former Fianna Fáil Taoiseach Charles Haughey and former Fine Gael minister Michael Lowry with Ben Dunne, a wealthy businessman. The McCracken Tribunal confirmed that:

* Haughey received over IR£1 million from Dunne and had evaded paying tax on these gifts;

- Lowry compromised his position as a minister and evaded tax by receiving payments from Dunne in various forms.

During the McCracken Tribunal, it emerged that offshore 'Ansbacher accounts' held in the Cayman Islands secretly benefited Haughey, but also some leading professional and business people. The Moriarty Tribunal (see below) was set up to investigate these offshore accounts.

The Flood Tribunal

The Flood Tribunal was established in October 1997 to investigate persistent and disturbing allegations of political corruption in the physical planning process. A particular focus was on decisions by local authorities to re-zone land from agricultural to industrial or housing use. By early 2001 it had established that:

- Dublin-based TDs and councillors accepted money from developers via a lobbyist;
- a senior local government official received a payment from developers to whom he gave 'advice';
- there was serious tax evasion by the official and the business people concerned;
- the Fianna Fáil minister responsible for broadcasting policy, Ray Burke, accepted a substantial 'election donation' from a radio entrepreneur.

The Moriarty Tribunal

Dáil Éireann set up the Moriarty Tribunal in September 1997. By early 2001 it had revealed that:

- Haughey received over IR£8.5 million from a wide range of private sources to finance an extravagant lifestyle;
- Denis Foley, a Fianna Fáil TD and Vice-Chairman of the Dáil PAC, was an Ansbacher account-holder;
- Haughey diverted parliamentary funds to personal use and to rescue the Fianna Fáil TD John Ellis from financial and political ruin.

The DIRT Inquiry

The deposit interest retention tax (DIRT) was imposed on interest paid by banks or building societies by the Finance Act 1986. In April 1998, there were press reports of bogus 'non-resident' bank accounts being used as a means of evading DIRT. The Dáil PAC, chaired by Fine Gael TD Jim Mitchell, looked into the matter. It found that:

- the main banks owed the state a substantial tax debt;

- the regulatory agencies had been negligent;
- successive Ministers for Finance were not involved in any wrongdoing;
- there was no political interference in the collection of DIRT.

Since the publication of the PAC report in December 1999, all the major financial institutions have made tax settlements with the Revenue Commissioners.

The causes of corruption

The incidents outlined above provide a broad basis for considering the causes of corruption in Ireland. In this section they are viewed in the light of:

- historical developments;
- longevity in power;
- increased state activity;
- ethical leadership;
- the financing of political parties;
- political career patterns.

Historical developments

Ireland has been independent since 1922, but corruption has a longer history. Nonetheless, most contemporary commentary has taken a rather too recent perspective. This has led to a view that Ireland's experience of corruption followed the change in the generations running the elite that occurred between 1957 and 1965. Many see a leadership struggle within Fianna Fáil in the 1960s as the marker for a fundamental change.

These 'sea change' accounts, which emphasise a radical turn of events, are persuasive in many respects. They neglect, however, the extent to which the civil service and, more particularly, local government had been in Irish hands for two decades before 1922. Further, the sea change approach fails to account for the resolute action that the first government of the Irish Free State had to take against local councils across its jurisdiction to counter widespread nepotism, jobbery and dubious financial dealings (see Chapter 4).

Longevity in power

When a political party has been in power for long periods, even – as with the Italian Christian Democrats – in coalitions, it may come to see its fortunes as interwoven with those of the institutions of government. In Ireland, the ascendancy of Fianna Fáil since the 1930s was effectively ended in 1989, when it accepted the role of being simply the senior partner in government. However, the party has been in power for most of the subsequent years, albeit as a result of coalition arrangements.

Appointees to state-sponsored companies have been at the centre of a number of the incidents of corruption. Some idea of the scale of government patronage can be gauged from the fact that more than 1,000 appointments were made to the boards of state agencies by the Fianna Fáil/PD government in the first thirty months after it assumed office in 1997. Even when membership of such boards may not be particularly remunerative, it can afford significant advantages in business intelligence and networking, and in bestowing a certain social status. For some, such appointments clearly also provided rent-seeking opportunities. The dangers are obvious: the authority to make appointments is a valuable political asset for ministers, and the longer a party holds office the greater will be the extent and penetration of its patronage.

Increased state activity

In common with other European countries, Ireland saw a major expansion in state activity in the course of the twentieth century. This trend has led to an expanded bureaucracy with increased discretionary powers, much of them exercised at local level through municipalities, health boards and decentralised offices. Many of the cases of fraud or embezzlement involving public servants arose from financial support regimes in agriculture, the licensing of vehicles, tax administration and the like.

Ethical leadership

Some observers have suggested that, in the Irish case, the propensity for corruption in these areas is augmented by a relatively relaxed level of taxation morality. On the issue of tax evasion, even when it is both financially significant and involves politicians, Irish people's judgement may well lack severity because petty transgressions are so widespread. Unethical behaviour, be it tax evasion, welfare fraud or false claims for compensation, is often defended because 'everybody does it', because 'the victims are usually faceless', or because the tax system is or was too onerous. The public judgement may be even less severe, it is suggested, if the victim is not just faceless but a remote agency of the EU.

Some explanations of corruption thus single out the lack of 'exemplary ethical leadership'. These suggest that corruption at elite level gives a signal to others that such behaviour is acceptable. This effect is hard to measure, but several incidents highlighted above suggest that very many people in politics and business must have been aware of the Ansbacher scheme for tax evasion and of other examples of dubious behaviour on the part of Ireland's senior leaders.

At a more general level, when Haughey was leader of Fianna Fáil, populist, short-term measures were often adopted in an *ad hoc* fashion, with little reference to proper procedure or broader policy considerations. In these circumstances, individual ministers, civil servants and business people may have been influenced by the perceived lax ethical standards in high places. The likelihood of decisive moral leadership may also have been inhibited because politicians in receipt of large sums from business occupied Cabinet positions, including of course that of Taoiseach.

The financing of political parties

One important theme in the comparative politics literature on corruption deserves special attention because of the frequency with which it seems to arise in the Irish case. This is the alleged link between corruption and the financing of political parties and elections.

Political parties need to finance major marketing operations, not just at election time but also to maintain a positive profile between formal campaigns. The decreasing role of both volunteer workers and individual member subscriptions has made parties more dependent on professional teams and capital-intensive campaign techniques. The frequency of elections and the level of intra-party competition between candidates of the same party for higher preference votes (see Chapter 2) exacerbate the problems of finance. In particular, they seem to have obliged election contenders to build up 'war chests' independently of their own party. Though the restrictions on election expenditure are now greater than in the 1980s and 1990s, the temptation to exceed the legal level is always there.

Many critics maintain that, in the absence of adequate state funding, the pressures of party competition create conditions that encourage a dependency on business and on wealthy individuals. Both Labour and Fine Gael have recently concluded that there ought to be a ban on corporate donations to political parties.

Political career patterns

The unfolding of the Foley case in 2000 demonstrated how a politician might be very much wealthier than his colleagues or electors imagined. According to a tabloid newspaper, *Ireland on Sunday*, most ordinary politicians are much richer than their salary scales suggest: 'one in every eight TDs is a millionaire'.[1] However, the examples given included some TDs whose 'valuation' included their principal residence as well as their assumed potential as heirs to business and other non-liquid assets. Moreover, the Irish system of public procurement, auditing and professional bureaucracy forecloses on most of the opportunities that politicians motivated to engage in illicit money-making – at either central or local government levels – might otherwise have. The crucial exception is in relation to planning. Be that as it may, the available evidence about Irish political career paths and corruption is too weak for generalisation.

The consequences of corruption in Ireland

Following Hope,[2] three types of consequences of corruption can be identified:

- economic;
- political;
- administrative.

Economic

There is a literature that suggests that corruption can have positive economic outcomes. Arguments favouring corruption are, however, disregarded here because they refer to political systems that are systemically corrupt or hopelessly inefficient.[3] The most direct economic consequence of corruption is to make business more costly. Rent-seeking by politicians or officials adds to the expense of business, diverts expenditure from other uses, increases taxes and causes macro-economic distortion. The allocation of local monopolies to suppliers of services with high initial costs, such as cable television, is fraught with economic dangers. Corruption may lead to the awarding of licences that are not justified on economic grounds; and customers and/or taxpayers eventually bear the cost.

One of a number of risk-assessment devices, the Corruption Perceptions Index, allows businesses to measure the perceived level of corruption in all the significant economies in the world. The Index suggests that the poorer the country, the more corrupt it is likely to be.[4] It represents, of course, an indirect measure of corruption, but it does allow Irish corruption to be placed in a comparative framework (see Table 6.3).

The cases of corruption that have arisen in Ireland rarely involved foreign companies or international trade. It may be that the position of multinational investors and businesses has been so strong that they have been able to resist rent-seeking demands from corrupt politicians or public servants. Alternatively such demands may simply not have been made. Interestingly, the international perception of Ireland's level of corruption does not seem to have altered significantly, despite recent revelations – although the impact on actual inward investment is impossible to assess in the absence of direct evidence from foreign companies.

Political

The second area of anxiety about the consequences of corruption is its impact on the political system itself. These may usefully be examined in terms of:

- public participation;
- political recruitment;
- political accountability.

Table 6.3. *Ranking of countries by the Corruption Perceptions Index, 1999*

Ranking	Country	Index score
1	Finland	10.0
2	Denmark	9.8
3	New Zealand	9.4
	Sweden	9.4
5	Canada	9.2
6	Iceland	9.1
	Norway	9.1
	Singapore	9.1
9	Netherlands	8.9
10	UK	8.7
11	Luxembourg	8.6
	Switzerland	8.6
13	Australia	8.3
14	United States	7.8
15	Austria	7.7
	Hong Kong	7.7
17	Germany	7.6
18	Chile	7.4
19	*Ireland*	*7.2*
20	Spain	7.0
21	France	6.7
22	Israel	6.6
23	Japan	6.4
	Portugal	6.4
25	Belgium	6.1

Scale: From 0 to 10 where '0' refers to a country in which business transactions are entirely penetrated by corruption, and '10' indicates a perfectly 'clean' country. In 2000, Ireland was nineteenth.
Source: Transparency International, see http://www.gwdg.de/~uwvw/2000Data.html.

Sustaining the political systems of liberal democracies depends in part on a relatively low level of actual citizen participation, but a high citizen belief in its potential efficacy. This rests in turn on significant levels of trust in politicians, public servants and other authority figures. In Ireland, trust in political institutions is relatively high. In the 1999 Spring Standard *Euro-barometer*, respondents in fifteen countries were asked to state their trust or distrust in their national and international institutions. On average, 35 per cent of Europeans trust the civil service, the Parliament, the government and the political parties of their country. The results show that average trust levels range from 25 per cent in Italy to 56 per cent in the Netherlands. The Irish score was 39 per cent. Yet, when disaggregated, it is clear that trust in the civil service (61 per cent) is much greater than in political parties (21 per cent).[5]

Perhaps a more telling indication of trust is the finding in April 2000 that 46 per cent of the respondents in an opinion poll indicated they did not believe a denial by Taoiseach Bertie Ahern that he received £50,000 from a businessman in 1989; while 36 per cent accepted Ahern's word, 18 per cent expressed no opinion. Interesting at the same time was that 67 per cent of those polled nonetheless approved of the Taoiseach's leadership.[6]

The primary agents for political recruitment in liberal democracies are political parties, and successful independent candidates are generally few. Of the candidates at the 1997 Irish general election, 21 per cent were independents but they secured just over 4 per cent of the seats.[7] Political parties generally recruit from a subset of their membership who are characterised by a willingness to stand, social circumstances that facilitate holding office and perhaps a number of other criteria that may be applicable to a particular constituency. In most countries, this has led to office holders being disproportionately male, middle aged and middle class, and from a relatively narrow range of professions. These international trends are mirrored in Ireland, but there is no evidence that corruption has affected the supply of potential political office holders.

With regard to the question of the effect of corruption on political accountability, we begin with Oireachtas members, who are of course answerable to the electorate. But Irish voters have been lenient, since few TDs touched by scandal have lost their seats. National odium has seldom overcome local loyalty; the clearest example of this arises from the case of Michael Lowry referred to above; he ran as an independent, against his former party, Fine Gael, and despite his national disgrace he won the seat.

Beyond direct answerability to the electorate, in the simple model of parliamentary accountability the focus for an assessment of corruption is properly the Oireachtas and its committees. In recognition of this, members of the Dáil and Seanad have a level of immunity from prosecution and, under Article 15.3 of Bunreacht na hÉireann, they cannot be sued for any remarks, comments or claims made in either house. Indeed, the Dáil itself is restricted in the action that it can take against its own members. For example, the Dáil was unable to suspend Liam Lawlor, TD, or apply any other sanction following his jailing in January 2001 for contempt (in the context of his lack of co-operation with the Flood Tribunal). Also interesting is that Ray Burke, in the case mentioned above, made his initial response to accusations of corruption in a statement on the floor of the Dáil.

Despite measures such as the Committees of the Houses of the Oireachtas (Compellability, Privileges and Immunities of Witnesses) Act 1997, critics suspect that the likelihood of corruption being detected is actually decreasing. In recognition of similar misgivings, many parliamentary systems augment the role of the legislature with other watchdog agencies such as ombudsmen, special prosecutors and other quasi-judicial bodies. In Ireland, it is a feature of several of the incidents cited above that Dáil TDs were unable to elicit crucial information which was later to be central to the outcomes of tribunals and other inquiries. The appointment of extra-parliamentary forums in the light of media revelations of corruption is a recognition that the established means of public accountability are deficient.

We move on now to the accountability of the members of the government. The doctrine of collective responsibility is supposed to make Cabinet colleagues sensitive to each other's decisions, each member being obliged publicly to defend every policy and action of the government. It is clear now that there were grounds for doubting the integrity of a recent Taoiseach, Charles Haughey, and other senior ministers; but their colleagues failed to act. The flaw may be the dominance of the Taoiseach in a Cabinet of career politicians. Alternatively, it may be that the pressure of individual departmental responsibilities did not allow time for a truly collective approach. Moreover, it is hardly in the interests of backbench parliamentarians from parties in government to question ministers so resolutely that they undermine their collective electoral credibility. Private party caucuses, therefore, assume a significant role in the system of parliamentary accountability. During Haughey's tenure as Taoiseach, party meetings were an important but obviously not sufficient check.

Administrative

After independence, the Free State bureaucracy retained the centralising features of its British predecessor. The enormous importance of the civil service and local authorities, and to a lesser extent the state-sponsored bodies, was heightened by the dominance of the public sector in the rather underdeveloped post-independence economy. Because of its political indispensability, the civil service was able to retain its corporate integrity and identity, and to resist pressures towards politicisation. As we have noted in Chapter 4, the recruitment and promotion procedures of the Irish public service are formally and rigorously meritocratic. Political appointments as special advisers to ministers are few in number and seldom controversial. And they end when governments change.

Traditionally, equity, impartiality and integrity have been key assets of the civil service. Today these are still important, but a number of other criteria have been identified as part of the NPM trend (see Chapter 4). It is widely recognised that the traditional management structure did not encourage individuals to take personal responsibility. NPM, by contrast, focuses on targets, performance indicators and payment by results. Some fear that this new environment will encourage some public servants to be less responsive to the traditional norms that inhibited corruption.

Partly as a safeguard against the abuse of bureaucratic power, several legislative changes have been made to the 1920s statutes that entrenched Ireland's British-style system of public administration. For example, in April 1998 the Freedom of Information Act came into effect. This gives public access to official records, files and reports of government departments and public bodies. The legislation effectively overturns the presumption that all official information is secret. Some data, especially commercially sensitive or legally privileged material, are excluded from the scope of the Act. Further, a Supreme Court decision, also in April 1998, widened the right of the media to report court cases and clarified the public's rights to information. The traditional safeguards have also been strengthened. To augment the established parliamentary process, the Office of the Ombudsman was established in 1980; it investigates complaints against a range of public authorities. Similarly, the C&A-G has been given wider powers in recent years to examine the effectiveness as well as the probity of public spending.

Though not strictly appropriate under this 'Administrative' heading, state–industry relations deserve a mention. The claim is that close relations between employers, trade unions and government blur the distinction between public and private interests, and may thus compromise political accountability and facilitate corruption. This danger has been recognised in corporatist institutional arrangements of the type found in several small European countries – which bring together business, labour and government in an effort to establish consensus on major economic policies. Corporatist agreements between the 'social partners' in Ireland are credited with underpinning economic growth (see Chapter 3). But what this means is that certain interest groups are afforded a direct role in political decisions not available to others. Corporatism also decreases the involvement of Parliament in policy formation and supervision. Further, ownership and direct supervision of certain enterprises by the state can compromise the neutrality of public officials, even in open democratic societies based on a predominantly market economy. Once more, however, there is no available evidence that corruption has arisen out of direct state involvement of this kind, or indeed out of Irish corporatism.

Issues and outcomes

Before turning to possible remedies for the kinds of corruption found in Ireland, it is useful to attempt to summarise the content and consequences of the cases that have occurred since the early 1990s. Tables 6.4 and 6.5 together represent an attempt to do that.

Table 6.4. *The Beef, McCracken, Moriarty and Flood Tribunals, and the DIRT Inquiry – issues and outcomes*

Instance	Issue	Outcome	Comment
Beef Tribunal (1994)	Government mishandles export procedures	Criminal charges, destabilised government	Followed UK media story
Lowry (1996)	Public duties, private interests	Resignation and inquiry	Followed media investigation
Haughey (1996)	Unethical receipt of money	Inquiry	Followed media investigation
Burke (1997)	Unethical receipt of money	Resignation and inquiry	Followed media investigation
AIB: bogus accounts (1998)	Evasion of DIRT	PAC inquiry	Followed media investigation
Flynn (1998)	Claims of unethical receipt of IR£50,000	Not reappointed as EU Commissioner; investigation by inquiry	Followed media investigation
Redmond (1999)	Unethical receipt of money	Tax investigation by Gardaí; investigation by inquiry	Followed revelations at Flood Tribunal
Ellis (1999)	Receipt of money from Haughey (out of party leader's account); bank writes off debt	Resignation as chair of Oireachtas committee; debate on treatment of debts of politicians by banks	Arose from Moriarty Tribunal
Foley (2000)	Ansbacher (offshore) account holder	Resignation as Vice-Chair and member of PAC; thirty-day suspension from Dáil	Arose from Moriarty Tribunal
Lawlor (2001)	Questionable receipt of money	Jailed for lack of cooperation	Arose from Flood Tribunal

Source: N. Collins and M. O'Shea, *Understanding Political Corruption in the Republic of Ireland*, Cork: Cork University Press, 2000.

Table 6.5. *Other illustrative 'corruption' incidents – issues and outcomes*

Instance	Issue	Outcome	Comment
Irish Sugar Company (1991)	Public duties and private interests	Resignation of chief executive	Increased awareness of public sector behaviour
Telecom Éireann (1991)	Public duties and private interests	Resignation of chair of the board	Increased reluctance of business elite to serve
Celtic Helicopters (1991)	Insider information	Weakened government reputation	Reinforced public disquiet
C&D Petfoods (1994)	Public duties and private interests	None (no resignation)	Taoiseach's judgement questioned
Coveney (1995)	Public duties and private interests	Demotion	Followed media story
Celtic Helicopters (1998)	Investment by individuals requested by Haughey	Departmental inquiry	McCracken and Moriarty Tribunals
Political parties (1998)	Political donations 'hidden' in company accounts – tax avoided	Revenue Commissioners' investigation	Followed media investigation
Sheedy affair (1998)	Unorthodox early release of prisoner	Inquiry by Chief Justice; resignations of judge and official	Followed media reporting and Dáil questions
Duffy (1999)	Public duties and private interests	Resignation as special adviser to Taoiseach	Followed media investigation
Harney and McCreevy (1999)	Acceptance of free holiday at French villa	No breach of Cabinet guidelines; public disquiet	Followed media investigation
Woodchester (1999)	Write-off of election debt of four senior Labour figures	Public focus on treatment by banks of politicians	Followed media investigation
O'Flaherty (2000)	Government nominee as Vice-President of European Investment Bank (after resignation as judge following the Sheedy affair)	Massive public disquiet; defeat for government in by-election; loss of support for coalition; nominee withdrew	Followed media reporting and Dáil questions

Source: N. Collins and M. O'Shea, *Understanding Political Corruption in the Republic of Ireland*, Cork: Cork University Press, 2000.

Anti-corruption strategies

Anti-corruption strategies are often influenced by the sense of scandal felt by the public about particular events. But Vito urges governments not to be fatalistic or passive about corruption.[8] With well focused and determined efforts, corruption can be reduced, though not to zero. Most Western anti-corruption strategies are based on more than one measure and they stress prevention. Ireland, for example, has subscribed to anti-corruption measures proposed by the World Trade Organisation, the World Bank, the International Monetary Fund and the Council of Europe, among others.

The analysis above suggests that corruption in Ireland is associated with discretion in public policies that allows particular and significant benefits to small numbers of individuals. One clear strategy, therefore, is to reduce the number of occasions on which discretion can be exercised. For example, governments will continue to make appointments that ensure that their political judgements are reflected in the major decisions of public bodies and that such appointments encourage some level of compliance with ministerial policy imperatives. But many of these appointments are already circumscribed by understandings with the social partners. It would be appropriate, then, to increase Dáil oversight through a process of parliamentary ratification such as occurs in the United States.

The case for increasing parliamentary oversight of policy as a counter to corruption was greatly helped by the role of the PAC in the DIRT Inquiry:

> Few countries in the world have investigated political corruption, maladministration and tax evasion with such zeal as Ireland is now doing.... At issue is public confidence in the integrity of our democracy.... The work of the Public Accounts Committee (PAC), in investigating the non-payment of DIRT taxes, has been critical in this regard.... [T]he PAC exposed tax evasion on a grand scale.[9]

The PAC was well resourced, cross-party in its make-up and narrowly focused. Any national strategy must therefore include steps to augment parliamentary oversight.

To enhance its own standing, the Dáil should place limits of various kinds on the 'outside' employment of ministers, senior civil servants and special advisers during, and for a period after, their tenure. It should also perhaps bar TDs from acting as lobbyists, even when this role is openly declared. Similarly, while the increased obligation to disclose personal assets has improved transparency, the Dáil should require the reporting of the *liabilities* of individual TDs – if not publicly, at least to some office in a position to 'blow the whistle' if conflicts of interest occur.

On the issue of confidentiality, the 1997 Freedom of Information Act is much less stringent than legislation currently in force elsewhere. In relation to central government, many public bodies, local authorities and health boards, it now gives public access to official records, files and reports. However, the Act's remit could be widened to cover other areas where officials or politicians exercise discretion over public resources. Some commercially sensitive or legally privileged material may have to remain excluded from the scope of the Act, but the rights of the public to information should be extended as far as possible.

Corporate funding of politics and political parties is another important issue. Garret FitzGerald, a former Taoiseach, points to some of the perceptions associated with this:

- business people may expect private benefit from contributions;
- public opinion is cynical about the motives of private contributors;
- politicians may avoid implementing policies to which contributors might be opposed.[10]

One oft-canvassed way of dealing with this problem would be to have public funding of political parties. Foreign experience suggests, however, that a completely publicly funded party system is hard to police. Further, it may reduce the independence of individuals or groups within parties who are out of step with the party leadership.

Recent tax evasion scandals have highlighted the problem of allowing professional groups to be self-regulating. Auditors and accountants are, like the judges, being asked to consider a new body with wider powers to oversee their operations, punish misconduct and offer a greater role to those outside the profession to investigate complaints. The new accountancy body would involve the state, but would remain responsible to the profession. It is possible, however, that the public may have lost patience with any substantial reliance on self-regulation of the professions.

An anti-corruption strategy at local government level would be required to recognise that the major source of disquiet is associated with planning and that this demands national action. Significantly, the Local Government Act 2000 provides for a strict ethics framework for councillors and local authority staff, especially in relation to planning. In most other areas of service delivery, priority could be given to increasing the consumer orientation of public services.

If a national anti-corruption strategy is to take on board the experience of recent tribunals, however, it must be based on a recognition that corruption is a constant danger and that *ad hoc* tribunals are an expensive and cumbersome instrument to counter the threat. An alternative might be a standing state anti-corruption agency, which would diagnose, and monitor for, signs of corruption in central and local government, health boards and other public sector organisations where the exercise of discretion, while necessary, may be open to abuse. Such a body could highlight areas vulnerable to corruption and thus inform the oversight of the Dáil itself and other regulatory agencies.

Conclusion

Corruption is an elusive phenomenon. Its measurement is at best indirect and tentative. In Ireland, however, it is difficult to remain sanguine in the face of the steady stream of revelations and accusations about the abuse of public office for private gain. In terms of the model used here, the conclusion of the analysis is that corruption in Ireland, while not systemic, is institutional:

- it is routine in some areas;
- in these, it occurs pervasively;
- weak or lax controls are associated with it;
- public trust in these areas is low.

In particular, corruption has been found:

- where politicians have a direct role in making specific, individual policy decisions of high value to wealthy business interests such as planning at local government level;
- where civil servants routinely exercise discretion over commercially valuable decisions in the context of lax systems of accountability and ambiguous policy objectives;
- where ministerial decisions are both commercially charged and the policy criteria insufficiently explicit.

Ireland has an important advantage in developing a counter-corruption strategy. Popular support for change is very high and the major political leaders, powerful private interests and key public servants all see reform as being in their interest. Any hint of tardiness is thus likely to prove unpopular. In contrast to systemically corrupt systems, the main political parties have more to gain from reform than continued corruption.

In the Irish cases outlined above, corruption is primarily associated with elected politicians rather than officials. This is not to discount possible corruption involving officials.[11] It is reasonable to assert, however, that the abuse of public office for private gain in Ireland is confined to a small minority of politicians and public officials.

Notes

1 J. Masterson, *Ireland on Sunday*, 27 February 2000.
2 K. R. Hope, 'Corruption and development in Africa', in K. R. Hope and B. Chicuto (eds), *Corruption and Development in Africa: Lessons from Country Care Studies*, Basingstoke: Macmillan, 2000.
3 Wei Shang-Jin, *Corruption in Economic Development: Beneficial Grease, Minor Annoyance, or Major Obstacle?*, Washington, DC: World Bank, Working Paper Series, 1999.

4 M. Wolf, *Financial Times*, 16 August 1997.
5 www.social-science-gesis.de/en/data_service/eurobarometer.
6 *Sunday Independent*, 30 April 2000.
7 T. Nealon, *Nealon's Guide to the 28th Dáil and Seanad: Election '97*, Dublin: Gill & Macmillan, 1997.
8 T. Vito, *Policies, Institutions and the Dark Side of Economics*, Cheltenham: Edward Elgar, 2000.
9 Editorial, *Sunday Independent*, 9 July 2000.
10 *Irish Times*, 17 January 1998.
11 In early 2001 an investigation began by all local authorities into the involvement of staff in helping people who were applying for planning permission for building work. It became clear fairly quickly that some local authorities' employees had been giving paid advice and providing the drawings required for planning submissions.

Further reading

Collins, N. and O'Shea, M., *Understanding Political Corruption in the Republic of Ireland*, Cork: Cork University Press, 2000.

della Porta, D. and Vannucci, A., *Corrupt Exchanges: Actors, Resources and Mechanisms of Political Corruption*, New York: Aldine De Gruyter, 1999.

Fiorentini, G. and Zamagni, S. (eds), *The Economics of Corruption and Illegal Markets*, Cheltenham: Edward Elgar, 1999.

Galtung, F., 'Criteria for sustainable corruption control', in A. K. Jain (ed.), *Economics of Corruption*, London: Kluwer Academic Publishers, 1998.

Klitgaard, R., 'International co-operation against corruption', 1997, at http://www.gwdg.de/~uwvw/research.htm.

Rose-Ackerman, S., *Corruption and Government*, Cambridge: Cambridge University Press, 1999.

7

Northern Ireland

If, as we have insisted, the Republic of Ireland can be understood by reference to the 'standard' analyses used by political scientists, we cannot say that with the same conviction about Northern Ireland. Not least of the reasons is that its politics and governance for the last thirty years have been characterised by enormous complexity and have been conducted in the shadow of violence and civil disorder.

Northern Ireland became a separate political entity in 1921, being one of the two Irish states that Britain's 1920 Government of Ireland Act was intended to create. 'Northern Ireland' was to consist of the six north-eastern counties[1] and 'Southern Ireland' the rest of the island. For a variety of reasons, but essentially because of the political and insurrectionist turmoil of the time, the Home Rule plan came into effect only in Northern Ireland, which, crucially, remained a part of the UK – now described as the United Kingdom of Great Britain and *Northern* Ireland, rather than of Great Britain and Ireland.

The Ulster Unionist Party had been founded to ensure the maintenance of the Union with Britain; its intention was to have the whole nine counties of the ancient Province of Ulster remain within the UK. Had this come to pass, however, Northern Ireland would have contained a precariously small majority of voters in favour of the Union – this calculation being based on the quite reasonable assumption that the great majority of Roman Catholics in Ulster would have preferred to be part of a united republican or Home Rule Ireland, whereas the overwhelming bulk of Protestants were in favour of partition and remaining within the Union. As a consequence, the three counties with a significant Catholic majority were excluded, with a view to balancing maximisation of Northern Ireland's land area with ensuring a permanent and secure unionist majority.[2] The Ulster Unionists were not particularly enthusiastic to begin with about the Home Rule mini-Parliament that had effectively been imposed on them; but with a virtual guarantee of continuous power, they took up the political reins in Northern Ireland, and enjoyed fifty years of uninterrupted one-party rule – that is, until the prorogation (or suspension) of the Northern Ireland Parliament in 1972.

Political and religious antagonisms in Northern Ireland have flared into civil disorder as well as violent action periodically since the IRA mounted its first offensive against the new Belfast regime in the early 1920s. On the whole, however, Unionist governments managed to repress dissent and to keep a generally firm grip on affairs until the late 1960s. To employ a mechanical analogy, Northern Ireland was maintained in a state of unstable equilibrium. This was occasionally disturbed, but was only finally upset when politics moved on to the streets in 1968. The current 'troubles' were precipitated initially by the failure of the liberal wing of the Unionist Party to persuade traditionalist colleagues that it was necessary to accede to at least some of the demands of the burgeoning civil rights movement – a conscious copy of the civil rights movement in the United States.

The Northern Ireland civil rights movement

These civil rights demands arose out of a perception – borne out to be correct by research undertaken since then – of determined discrimination against Catholics down through the years, in almost all areas of social and economic life.[3] Various reforms were demanded:

- a fairer system for the allocation of public housing (houses built for rent by local government bodies), which was in high demand;
- the extension of the local government franchise from 'householders' (those who owned or rented houses) to *all* adults, together with the elimination of multiple voting rights based on ownership of property these two claims being jointly encapsulated in the slogan 'one man one vote';
- an end to the gerrymandering, which involved the manipulation of constituency geographical boundaries to ensure continuing unionist domination in key local government areas which might otherwise have been expected to be in nationalist hands;
- legislation to ensure fair and equal employment opportunities for all.

To begin with, the civil rights movement drew support from a wide political base, including many people from a unionist background. In part this cross-community support was a consequence of the principal demands of the movement being for rights (enumerated above) which citizens in the rest of the UK already enjoyed. Despite that, the Northern Ireland government claimed that 'civil rights' were simply a new cover for nationalist agitation and that the Union with Britain was thus threatened.[4] Although the Protestant working class endured many of the same political, economic and social disadvantages as their Catholic counterparts, most ordinary Protestants accepted the government's interpretation of the protests as a nationalist/republican plot. The mainly Protestant police force – the Royal Ulster Constabulary (RUC) – was thus deployed to maintain order: marches and meetings were broken up, and the police were sometimes seen to be cooperating with Protestant counter-protesters.

During 1969 a number of major stand-offs between civil rights demonstrators and the RUC occurred simultaneously across Northern Ireland, which stretched the force to breaking point. The British government was finally forced to intervene and troops trained for battle rather than civil disorder were put on the streets in large numbers. In the period that followed, the UK government in London – which of course remained the sovereign power – continued to put pressure on the Unionists for reforms. As a result, several important concessions were made to the civil rights movement's demands. A step too far for the Unionist government of Northern Ireland, however, was a proposal that all responsibility for security, and law and order in general, be taken over by London. Unionist defiance in face of this brought about the prorogation (or suspension) of Northern Ireland's Parliament and government in March 1972. From then until 1999, apart from a short interregnum in 1974, 'direct rule' from London passed into the charge of a member of the UK Cabinet, the Secretary of State for Northern Ireland.

Violence takes over

In the meantime the almost entirely peaceful protests of the civil rights movement had been overtaken by a major surge of violence initiated principally by a rejuvenated 'Provisional' IRA. The IRA had called off its previous armed campaign, which lasted from 1956 to 1962, first because it was failing to engender much support among the nationalist people in Northern Ireland; and second because the IRA and its Sinn Féin political wing were moving in a fashionably leftist direction and were beginning to question the value of armed action in pursuit of a united socialist Ireland. In 1969, following internal dissention, the IRA and Sinn Féin split into 'Official' and 'Provisional' versions:

> [The Provisional IRA] was not simply another manifestation of armed republicanism. It was born following loyalist attacks on the Catholic ghettoes of west Belfast in August 1969. Its personnel were the young people of those areas intent upon defending themselves. The graffiti of the time – 'IRA = I Ran Away' captures the sense of despair felt by many residents who believed that the old IRA leadership was more intent on conducting seminars in Marxist theory rather than looking after their own. The new breed were more indigenous and more ruthless.[5]

The Official IRA called a cease-fire in the early 1970s, and for all practical purposes faded from view, while Official Sinn Féin transformed itself over the years into a left-wing grouping, the Workers' Party, committed to struggle for a united socialist Ireland by means of the ballot box.

However, there was early confirmation of the ruthlessness of the Provisional IRA. Following more than 300 bombing incidents attributable to its volunteers in the first seven months of 1971, in August the British government finally succumbed to the clamour for the introduction of internment (or imprisonment without trial) of terrorist suspects. Based on deeply flawed and out-of-date intelligence, some 350 or so people were arrested in overnight army raids. In the end, 240 people were locked up without benefit of court procedures, some of them following brutal interrogation. Cutting a long story short, internment was a disaster, and rather than rendering the IRA less effective, recruits poured into the organisation and nationalist sympathies began to lean much more than before in a republican direction.

What drove the IRA's revived campaign? The first reason was the defensive one already referred to. Second, however, the campaign was also opportunistic, to the extent that the disorder on the streets had created circumstances more conducive to the conduct of a paramilitary campaign. Third, the responses and reactions to the campaign by the British government, the RUC and the troops often helped swell the ranks of IRA volunteers. Aside from internment itself, the most potent example of the forces of the state acting as an unwitting recruiting agent for the IRA was Bloody Sunday in Derry/Londonderry in 1972, when thirteen unarmed civilians were shot dead by paratroopers during a banned civil rights march. Another powerful example was the British government's refusal in 1981 to bow to any of the demands of prisoners on hunger strike for what they called 'political status'; ten prisoners starved themselves to death before the action was called off. Finally, however, the fundamental drive behind the IRA's campaign remained the same as it had always been: to remove the 'British presence' and thus end the illegitimate partition of Ireland.

In seeming fulfilment of the predictions of those unionists who saw 'civil rights' as a coded euphemism for Irish nationalism, the campaign intended to achieve 'British rights' for the citizens of Northern Ireland was thus overwhelmed by a paramilitary crusade to eliminate the British state from Northern Ireland. Acting in Britain (almost exclusively in England) as well as in Northern Ireland, the IRA's 'armed struggle' consisted of two main components: first, the bombing of 'economic targets' – restoration or replacement of which would be of significant cost to the British government; and second, the killing, by a variety of means, of serving and former soldiers and police officers, politicians and British royalty. It needs to be added that there was sometimes a calculated sectarian element in IRA activity – including the killing of uninvolved Protestants, using cover names such as the 'Catholic Action Force'.

Predominantly as a reaction to the IRA's campaign, two paramilitary organisations loyal to the Union with Britain, the Ulster Volunteer Force (UVF) and the Ulster Defence Association (UDA), engaged in a counter-campaign, which consisted in the main of the random assassination of innocent, un-involved Catholics. By 1994, when the IRA, UDA and UVF cease-fires were called, the 'troubles' in Northern Ireland had claimed more than 3,000 lives – military, paramilitary and civilian – and caused over 30,000 injuries.

Religion and political division

Discussion of the politics of Northern Ireland is often expressed in religious terms which seem anachronistic to the outsider. It will be useful, therefore, before going on to describe Northern Ireland's institutional structures, to discuss briefly the nature of the division.

The roots of the problem in Northern Ireland can be traced to the dif-ferential success of colonial policy in Ireland. As was noted in Chapter 1, plantation was the means by which British rule was established. An effort was made to uproot one group of people, the native Catholics, and replace them with English and Scottish Protestants whose loyalty to the British Crown was assured. The Province of Ulster was always very different from the rest of Ireland and the greater success of this policy in the north-east set Ulster even further apart. Plantation began in earnest in 1607 and was largely over by 1641; but it plainly established the current pattern of social, religious, pol-itical and economic division. It is broadly true that there are still two camps and the rallying calls of the main political forces thus tend to appeal to each community separately.

The Protestants

The Protestant majority in Northern Ireland belongs to a number of denom-inations, the two largest being the Presbyterian Church in Ireland (which has some Scottish associations) and the Church of Ireland (the Irish branch of the Anglican/Episcopalian family). Methodism too has a significant presence, but there are also a large number of 'independent' and 'fundamentalist' Prot-estant churches, some of which claim the allegiance of no more than a few hundred people. For many of these fundamentalists, Northern Ireland is the last bastion of the true tradition of the Christian Reformation. For loyalists – the name generally used to describe the most militant advocates of the main-tenance of the Union – the link with the British Crown is also a guarantee of Protestant hegemony, which could not of course be sustained in an overwhelmingly Catholic united Irish state. The Orange Order, a religious-cum-political organisation to which many Unionist politicians belong, epitomises these values.

The great bulk of unionist-minded people, on the other hand, wish to remain in the UK for economic and sentimental rather than religious reasons. They want the British government's large financial subvention, which until recently ensured that living standards were generally higher in Northern Ireland than in the Republic, to be maintained. They also wish to retain their links to the wider British community, with its cultural traditions, its liberal democratic institutions, the Queen, the Union flag and the Commonwealth. Moreover, a significant number of such people have come to consider the fifty years of Home Rule in Northern Ireland a mistake.

Their argument is that this was bound to exacerbate community divisions by making politics almost entirely about partition. A few have followed the logic of this position to its conclusion and have come to favour fully 're-integrating' Northern Ireland into the UK – seeking a return to the way Ireland was governed, directly from Westminster, before partition. Northern Ireland would thus be governed 'like Yorkshire', with British national political parties – principally the Conservatives, Liberal Democrats and Labour – organising and fighting elections for the Northern Ireland seats in the House of Commons in London. A linked effect, it has been argued, is that 'normal' left/right politics would develop under this scenario. Given that the local Parliament at Stormont (on the outskirts of Belfast) was seen to have become one of the mechanisms for division, an essential concomitant of the 'integrationist' view is that there ought to be no more than low-level government institutions based in Northern Ireland itself.

The Catholics

The Catholic community forms just over 40 per cent of the population of Northern Ireland. It is, like its Protestant counterpart, divided by class and other social distinctions; for while Catholics suffer a disproportionate share of disadvantage, most are neither marginalised nor deprived, and the Catholic middle class has grown considerably in the last thirty years. In religious terms Roman Catholicism also has its fundamentalists, and it is possible to detect a progressive/conservative divide, especially since the 1960s, when the Church's Second Vatican Council began to erode old doctrinal certainties. However, this has had no discernible effect on the politics of Northern Ireland. In political terms, while there is a traditional and enduring link between being a Catholic and being a nationalist, opinion polls have always indicated that significant numbers of Catholics are content for the Union with Britain to remain. What really unites Catholics, of all political dispositions and complexions, is mistrust of Unionism – based on being at the hard end of fifty years of devolved government in Northern Ireland.

Integration and education

Day to day, each community is generally self-sufficient in social and cultural terms, and contact with the 'other side' is often perfunctory in both these respects. However, while a few workplaces are segregated, it is in a workplace setting that most intercommunal contact takes place – and this is usually harmonious.

Significantly, the great majority of Catholic children attend schools run under the auspices of the Roman Catholic Church – schools whose ethos is clearly denominational and often Irish in cultural outlook. Until recently, the price to the Catholic community of such separate educational provision was that it had itself to raise a small proportion of the capital costs involved in building schools. However, the UK government now meets in full both running costs and capital investment.

State schools are, for all practical purposes, Protestant schools. Local Protestant clergy are entitled to be represented on their boards of governors and the schools reflect – for the most part – a self-consciously British outlook. Barriers between the two school systems have been broken down to a limited extent by government-funded initiatives like the Education for Mutual Understanding and Cultural Heritage programmes. The UK government has also provided special funding for the development of religiously 'integrated' education and, while still few in number, there are now integrated schools in all the main centres of population.

Catholic disadvantage

Since the Unionists saw it as their central task to defend Protestant interests, it was the clear objective of both the central Northern Ireland government and local councils after 1922 to keep Catholics in an inferior economic position. In particular, it was necessary to prevent them from gaining a foothold in positions of political or administrative influence. As the then Prime Minister, Sir James Craig, notoriously reported to the Northern Ireland House of Commons in 1934: 'all I boast is that we are a Protestant Parliament and a Protestant State'.[6]

Unemployment in Northern Ireland has almost always run at higher levels than in the rest of the UK and has been consistently at its worst in places where Catholics form a greater than average proportion of the population. For example, a historically lower level of industrial development left much of the west of Northern Ireland, where Catholics are in the majority, relatively deprived of job opportunities, in all sectors of the labour market. Although there is little evidence to support the contention that standard government economic development schemes were administered so as to ensure greater employment in Protestant areas, it is clear that the decision in the 1960s to site a new city (Craigavon) in the south-east, rather than develop the existing north-western city of Derry, was motivated by fear that more Catholics than Protestants would have benefited from the latter.

The available figures down the years support the claim of serious Catholic disadvantage. For example, in 1971 Catholic unemployment was 13.9 per cent while the Protestant figure was 5.6 per cent. Catholics were also more likely to be found in occupations which experienced the highest rates of seasonal and long-term unemployment. Despite the British government's Fair Employment Act 1976, and the major amendments made to it by the 1989 Act of the same name – which now provide Northern Ireland with the most forceful anti-discrimination legislation in Europe – the situation has not changed substantially since then. Despite a fall in unemployment levels in the late 1990s, Catholics are still more than twice as likely to be unemployed as Protestants; while Catholic representation in the civil and public services generally is now 'correct' in proportional terms, Catholics are still under-represented at the most senior levels; and the same is true as regards higher management positions in the private sector. Instead, what might be described as the Catholic upper middle classes are found disproportionately in the liberal professions such as the law and medicine, where entry is largely determined by educational achievement.

As to why there has been so little change in the situation in the last twenty years, the much higher unemployment figures of the early 1990s suggest a major part of the explanation must lie in that period of economic decline. Eliminating an imbalance not only requires new jobs but also a turnover of personnel in existing jobs – which does not happen when opportunities for mobility in the labour market are scarce. However, it seems reasonable to expect that recent advances on the job opportunities front will begin to feed through to the employment figures in the fairly near future.

The most obvious physical manifestation of community division is segregated housing. There is a strong tradition of public provision of housing in Northern Ireland, traceable mainly, though not entirely, to the beginnings of the welfare state in the UK in the 1940s. But for reasons of electoral advantage and social control, council houses – houses built and owned by local government bodies, for rent to those who could not afford to buy their own home – were often allocated on a sectarian basis. Indeed, if Northern Ireland in the 1960s had the worst housing conditions in the UK, this was not entirely due to lack of resources. Londonderry Corporation (the then city council) actually refused to build any houses at all in the mid-1960s, because while the available land was in Unionist/Protestant-controlled electoral wards, the most likely tenants would have been Catholics.

Against this background, one of the civil rights demands acceded to relatively quickly was the removal of housing functions from local authorities. An independent Housing Executive assumed these instead, and since the outbreak of the 'troubles' the housing stock has undergone remarkable improvement. That said, the segregation of working-class areas on sectarian lines has actually increased in the last thirty years, as members of each community have sought safety in numbers. On the other hand, with the major exception of Derry, where the River Foyle has come to form a major sectarian frontier, middle-class housing has generally remained integrated.

Parties and elections in Northern Ireland

From 1922 onwards, the position of Northern Ireland within the UK – 'the constitutional issue' – dominated politics; but the sides in this argument were, and are, internally divided. Dealing first with parties in favour of the Union with Britain, the Ulster Unionist Party (UUP) is not only the strongest party but also the oldest; and it held power in Northern Ireland continuously from 1921 until 1972. The Democratic Unionist Party (DUP) is more populist in approach and was formed in 1971 by fundamentalist Protestants who felt that the UUP was insufficiently resolute in defending the Union. Although these two parties cooperate from time to time, relationships have often been strained because of the very different styles of their respective leaderships. The United Kingdom Unionist Party (UKUP) was formed by the MP for North Down in 1995; it sought the 'reintegration' of Northern Ireland into the UK governmental system (see above); but it split into two warring factions in 1998.

The Progressive Unionist Party (PUP) and the Ulster Democratic Party (UDP) have received much attention since the 1994 paramilitary cease-fires (see below). They have their roots in the UVF and UDA respectively. The PUP and UDP are generally leftist/populist in political approach, having come to regard the two main unionist parties as inherently unable to look after the economic and social interests of working-class Protestants. Tracking closely the changing postures of their paramilitary counterparts, the PUP and UDP have worked jointly from time to time. However, in mid-2000 these parties moved far apart, echoing a murderous tit-for-tat dispute between the UDA and the UVF in the loyalist Shankill Road in Belfast.

'In the middle', together with some smaller groupings, is the Alliance Party. It was formed in 1970 to bring Protestants and Catholics together in order to reach an agreed settlement of the Northern Ireland problem, preferably within the Union, and has intermittently attracted a substantial middle-class vote. Anecdotal evidence suggests that it attracts more Catholic than Protestant support. It should be mentioned in passing that the political left too has generally taken a 'middle' view on the constitutional issue. But the labour tradition has enjoyed only intermittent electoral success down the years.[7] In the 1996 Peace Forum elections (see below) the four declaredly left-wing groupings together gained only 1.5 per cent of the vote.

Also set up in 1970, after the effective demise of the old Nationalist Party, was the Social Democratic and Labour Party (SDLP). Since then it has become the largest nationalist-minded party and unlike Sinn Féin, its main rival for nationalist votes, the SDLP has always been firmly committed to peaceful democratic methods. Sinn Féin, which is closely linked with the IRA and is often described as the political wing of the republican movement, has a much longer history and is more ardently nationalist than the SDLP. Until recently, like the IRA, it endorsed the use of force in the pursuit of a united all-Ireland

Table 7.1. *Results of the 1996 elections to the Northern Ireland Peace Forum*

Party name	No. of votes	% vote
Ulster Unionist Party (UUP)	181,829	24.2
Social Democratic and Labour Party (SDLP)	160,786	21.4
Democratic Unionist Party (DUP)	141,413	18.8
Sinn Féin	116,377	15.5
Alliance Party	49,176	6.5
United Kingdom Unionist Party (UKUP)	27,774	3.7
Progressive Unionist Party (PUP)	26,082	3.5
Ulster Democratic Party (UDP)	16,715	2.2
Conservative Party	3,595	0.5
Others	27,595	3.8

Source: Based on local newspaper reports of results.

state. After the IRA cease-fire of August 1994, however, it began to distance itself, albeit somewhat tentatively, from the 'armed struggle'.

The results of the 1996 election to choose members of the Northern Ireland Peace Forum provide the best overall picture of the distribution of votes in all electoral contests in the 1990s – see Table 7.1. It was from among those elected to the Forum that negotiating teams for the associated multi-party peace talks (see below) were chosen. Compared with the 1992 Westminster general election, the main gainers were the DUP and Sinn Féin; and the main losers were the UUP, Conservatives and Alliance. That there was virtually no crossing of the great divide is shown by the fact that in percentage terms the total unionist vote remained firmly in the mid-fifties, while that of the nationalists stayed equally firmly in the mid-thirties. In the Westminster general election of May 1997 Sinn Féin again did well; it increased its vote in all the constituencies which it fought, actually improving slightly on its Forum performance; and it succeeded in taking two of Northern Ireland's eighteen seats in the House of Commons by having leader Gerry Adams and his close associate Martin McGuinness returned as MPs – for West Belfast and West Tyrone respectively.[8]

The economy and industry in Northern Ireland

Northern Ireland has for many years been characterised as a 'dependent economy': dependent on external funding, external ideas and external initiatives.[9] It is true that the public sector still accounts for more than 30 per cent of those in employment and public expenditure per capita in Northern Ireland remains above the UK average. However, two other things need to be said about this. First, the dependency thesis relies on viewing Northern

Ireland as an economic entity in its own right rather than as a component part of the wider UK economy – an economy that plainly includes several other deprived areas in receipt of significant subventions from central government funds. Second, there is clear evidence in 2001 that the overall situation is improving, with Northern Ireland beginning to enjoy an economic growth rate higher than that in the rest of the UK – albeit one still lower than that in the Republic.

Northern Ireland began by being the most economically successful and industrialised part of the island, but the seeds of a long-term decline in its staple industries – linen, shipbuilding and general engineering – had already been sown in the early years of the twentieth century. By the late 1950s the economy was in serious difficulties and, like its counterpart in Dublin, the Northern Ireland government began to look abroad for investors. A particular success was in the man-made fibre industry. Six major multinationals were persuaded to invest in manufacturing plants, which came to employ many thousands of workers. Sadly, this was a short-lived phenomenon and the industry collapsed in the early 1980s in face of cheaper supplies from low-wage, newly industrialised countries. International competition – or 'globalisation' – together with various economic shocks also had depressing effects on other sectors: woven textiles, clothing, tyre manufacture and tobacco products. But while new 'high-tech' ventures have begun to make a significant contribution to employment, the encouragement of local small enterprise has been effective only at the margins.

The result of all this is that despite starting from very different positions three-quarters of a century ago, Northern Ireland and the Republic presently stand at close to the same point on a range of economic indicators – with the Republic a short head in front on most of these.[10] The underlying picture is of course more complex than that generalisation would suggest. But surely the most remarkable statistic is that while almost half the Northern Ireland workforce in the 1920s was engaged in industrial occupations, the figure today hovers around 25 per cent.

As in the Republic, agriculture and food production remain important industries in Northern Ireland. In terms of wealth creation, they have also been among the best-performing sectors, with annual gross outputs of between £1,700 and £2,000 million. Over 60 per cent of what is produced is exported and some 15–20 per cent of Northern Ireland's workforce is engaged, directly or indirectly, in agriculture. However, as elsewhere in the UK, the late 1990s saw a serious deterioration in the food sector and farm incomes declined steeply. Indeed, an increasing proportion of the rural labour force is no longer engaged full time in agricultural production and farm household incomes often depend to a significant extent on non-agricultural employment.

Although somewhat later than the rest of the UK, Northern Ireland was subjected to the rigours of Conservative economic policy. In particular, these involved privatisation (the sale of state-owned companies into the private sector) and open competitive tendering (or bidding) for services formerly provided from within the public sector. The two major engineering operations remaining in Belfast, the Harland & Wolff shipyard and Shorts' aircraft and armaments plants, both in public ownership for many years, were privatised. So too were Belfast International Airport and Northern Ireland Electricity (the latter having first been broken up into separate generating and distribution companies). Water supply and public transport must surely soon be candidates for the same treatment.

In broader terms, a lack of jobs was – and arguably remains – Northern Ireland's greatest scourge. The unemployment rate in the mid-1990s was running at between 13 and 14 per cent, compared with around 7 per cent in Britain; but some areas – West Belfast, Cookstown, parts of Strabane and Derry – reported pockets of male unemployment of more than 50 per cent; and over half of those unemployed had been so for over a year (which compares with 35–40 per cent in the UK as a whole). By early 2001, however, average unemployment in Northern Ireland had fallen to less than 6 per cent, and there had even been some improvement in the worst black spots – for example, in Strabane the rate had fallen from over 20 per cent in the early 1990s to less than 10 per cent at the end of the decade.

The institutions of government

As a result of the Government of Ireland Act 1920, in 1921 a wide range of responsibilities – education, health, personal social services, home affairs (including law and order), housing, planning, labour market issues and economic development – were devolved to the regional Parliament and government in Belfast. Responsibility for certain other matters, such as foreign affairs, defence, taxation and the postal service, were reserved to the sovereign Parliament in London, and continued to be administered in Northern Ireland by UK civil servants. However, a separate civil service – the Northern Ireland Civil Service (NICS) – was set up to administer the devolved functions.

This arrangement survived until 1972, when the Northern Ireland Parliament was prorogued. Under the new 'direct rule' arrangements, the NICS remained in place, but the new Secretary of State for Northern Ireland and a number of junior ministers in a newly formed British government department named the Northern Ireland Office (NIO) took over direction of the work of the former Northern Ireland government departments. One significant one, the Ministry of Home Affairs (in effect the Ministry of Justice), was abolished and the NIO itself (supported by UK civil servants rather than NICS staff) assumed full responsibility for the contentious area of law and order. It was inevitable also that the NIO would become responsible for what came to be labelled 'political development' – the search for a long-term solution to the Northern Ireland problem.

However, direct rule from Westminster did little to disturb the fundamentals of the machinery of government and the mode of delivery of public services until the late 1990s, except as regards the legislative process. Whereas the law in Northern Ireland in respect of devolved matters had been a matter almost entirely for the Northern Ireland Parliament prior to 1972, from then on legislation was enacted in three different ways. First, bills passed by Parliament at Westminster could be declared to have effect throughout the UK – in other words, to apply in Northern Ireland as well as England, Scotland and Wales. Second, important bills that affected Northern Ireland alone could be dealt with using the full procedures of both houses. This was, however, an extremely rare event. It became more usual to legislate on Northern Ireland matters using a third method, called Orders in Council. Since debate was very restricted, and it was not possible for amendments to be proposed to such an Order, the process was the subject of frequent complaint by MPs from Northern Ireland and their parliamentary allies.

A further institution was added to existing structures following the Anglo-Irish Agreement of 1985 (which is further discussed below). It established the Intergovernmental Conference: a mechanism by which the government of the Republic was entitled to put forward its views on a range of matters affecting the government of Northern Ireland. The Conference, which had a secretariat in Belfast staffed by both UK and Irish civil servants, met regularly and was chaired jointly by the Secretary of State for Northern Ireland and the Irish Minister for Foreign Affairs. Dominating the Conference's agenda until the early 1990s were three particular issues: the extradition of terrorist suspects from one jurisdiction to another; increasing the confidence of nationalists in the administration of justice in Northern Ireland; and addressing the disadvantage which Catholics suffered in the labour market. Following the 'Downing Street Declaration' of December 1993, however, virtually all of the Conference's attention was diverted to the 'peace process'. If the day-to-day operation of governmental procedures, as well as the management of these, was little affected by the imposition of direct rule from London, the structure of government was to be altered radically by the Belfast 'Good Friday' Agreement (on which see more below).

By the mid-1980s the number of Northern Ireland departments had been reduced by the NIO from a high of nine in the early 1970s to just six – the work of which included supervision of a number of semi-autonomous and elected bodies with sub-regional and local responsibilities. But in order to create sufficient posts to ensure adequate representation of the various local political parties at ministerial level under the 1998 Good Friday Agreement, the number was increased to ten, by a rejigging of existing responsibilities and the introduction of some new ones. The party of the minister heading each department when the Executive was first set up is given in square brackets after the departmental name.

(1) As might be expected, the *Department of Agriculture and Rural Development* [SDLP Minister] has in its care matters pertaining to food, food safety, farming and environmental policy. It is also responsible for: agri-food and agri-business affairs; veterinary provision, including animal health; forestry; rivers; and sea fisheries. Significant is the Department's link with the new Foyle, Carlingford and Irish Lights Commission, a cross-border implementation body set up under the Good Friday Agreement.

(2) The *Department of Culture, Arts and Leisure* [UUP Minister] is an almost entirely new creature. As well as oversight of some existing bodies, such as the Ordnance Survey (the public map-making body) and the Public Record Office (which maintains historical documentary records), it has assumed several innovative duties: in respect of publicly sponsored events, inland fisheries and waterways, and policy on the use of the Irish and Ulster-Scots languages. The last two of these are associated with all-Ireland implementation bodies: the Waterways Board, and the North–South Language Body (translated as An Foras Teanga in Irish, and as Tha Boord o'Leid in Ulster-Scots).

(3) The new *Department of Education* [Sinn Féin Minister] has lost most of the further and higher education functions of its predecessor. It has oversight of the five education and library boards, whose task is day-to-day educational provision at nursery (pre-school), primary and secondary levels. It also supports financially three independent bodies: the council responsible for the maintenance of educational standards; the Council for Catholic Maintained Schools, the employing authority for teachers in Catholic schools; and the Council for Integrated Education, which promotes the development of religiously integrated schools.

(4) The *Department of Enterprise, Trade and Investment* [UUP Minister] also has fewer functions than its Economic Development predecessor – being almost entirely focused on generating job growth. It delivers this with the support of four semi-independent bodies, with responsibility for encouraging foreign direct investment, the development of local small enterprises (these first two were to be merged in mid-2001), technological research and tourism. The Department is also linked with two cross-border implementation bodies, concerned with trade and business development and special EU programmes.

(5) The *Department of the Environment* [UUP Minister] has taken on many of the tasks of its predecessor of the same name, with the important exception of the development of policy on public housing. Its responsibilities include: environmental planning control; protection of heritage, wildlife and the countryside; driver and vehicle testing and licensing; road safety; waste management; and central oversight of elected local councils.

(6) The *Department of Finance and Personnel* [SDLP Minister] has inherited all but a few of the functions of its similarly named predecessor. The pivotal, 'purse-strings' department, it has the 'Treasury' or 'Exchequer' role, as well

as responsibility for the management of the NICS. It also collects the very small amounts arising from locally imposed taxation – mainly value-related property 'rates'. Indeed, it is necessary to emphasise here that the British Treasury, responsible to Parliament at Westminster, retains complete control over fiscal policy across the UK. As a result, the two most important functions of Finance and Personnel are to negotiate the maximum possible allocation of funds from the Treasury in London; and to distribute these to the Northern Ireland Departments in a fair and defensible manner.

(7) The *Department of Health, Social Services and Public Safety* [Sinn Féin Minister] has the same overall responsibility for health and social services as its predecessor; it also has the central supervisory role in respect of the sub-regional health and social services boards. However, it has lost the management of the social security system and gained a broad public safety remit, including ambulance and fire services. A cross-border implementation body, the Food Safety Promotion Board, is linked to the Department.

(8) The new *Department of Higher and Further Education, Training and Employment* [SDLP Minister] has inherited functions from two previous departments. From Education it has taken on tertiary (college and university) education, while from Economic Development it has inherited a mixed bag of employment-related services: job markets; vocational training; employment law; and industrial relations.

(9) The *Department for Regional Development* [DUP Minister] has taken on two functions previously undertaken by Environment, namely transport and water. It is responsible, first, for strategic transport planning, provision and maintenance of roads, and policy-making in respect of railways, buses, ports and airports. Second, it has a duty to ensure a safe, potable and sufficient water supply, as well as adequate drainage and sewerage services.

(10) As well as inheriting responsibility from Environment for policy on urban regeneration, housing and land use, the *Department for Social Development* [DUP Minister] has also taken on duties in respect of community development, child support, social legislation, social welfare and – most important of all – social security.

Most of the cross-border implementation bodies came formally into being on 2 December 1999, and are intended to implement policies agreed by appropriate ministers in both Northern Ireland and the Republic. The bodies are funded by financial grants from the 'sponsoring' ministries, and they will eventually be staffed by a combination of civil servants (transferred or seconded from their parent departments on either side of the border) and directly recruited staff. With the agreement of the Northern Ireland Assembly and the Oireachtas in Dublin, it will be possible to set up further implementation bodies in the future, in areas already identified as possibilities for useful North–South cooperation.

In conclusion, it could hardly be argued that the new departmental structures in Northern Ireland and their associated cross-border bodies accord with standard models of rational administration. However, as we shall see, the quest for the most efficient and effective way of organising the conduct of government business has taken second place to the political demands of the peace process.

Local government

Intended primarily to remove contentious matters such as housing from the local council arena, the Local Government (Northern Ireland) Act 1972 provided for the creation of twenty-six local authorities with responsibilities for relatively few executive functions – certainly by comparison with the rest of the UK and the Republic of Ireland. These include certain regulatory services, such as cinema licensing, building regulations and health inspection. Councils also provide a number of direct services to the public: street cleaning; refuse collection and disposal; burial grounds and crematoria; public baths; culture and recreation facilities; and tourist amenities. Added to these in the early 1990s was some limited freedom to promote local industrial development.

Refuse collection and disposal and leisure and community services represent the only major items of expenditure by local authorities in Northern Ireland. In consequence, local government is responsible for less than 3 per cent of total public expenditure. Local authorities were also entitled at one time to representation on the management boards of certain public agencies, on a range of advisory councils and on the area boards responsible for health and education provision. However, as in the rest of the UK, the Conservative government reduced such representation over the years and replaced nominees of local councils by business people. Finally, local councils are consulted too about matters for which they have no direct responsibility, such as proposed house-building schemes, planning applications and road developments within their area.

Elections to the twenty-six local authorities are held every four years. The 1993 contest was an almost perfect rerun of that in 1989, leaving eighteen councils in the control of parties in favour of the Union with Britain. The UUP took 29 per cent of the total vote, the SDLP 22 per cent, the DUP 17 per cent, Sinn Féin 12 per cent, the Alliance 8 per cent and 'others' 12 per cent. However, that picture changed somewhat in 1997. The SDLP's share dropped a little, to just under 21 per cent, but Sinn Féin improved its showing by nearly 5 per cent to reach an all-time high of almost 17 per cent, confirming that it had become the third largest party in Northern Ireland.

The unionist parties seem to have failed to get their voters out: the UUP dropped back by over 1 per cent to below 28 per cent, and the DUP by roughly the same amount to just over 15 per cent, while Alliance also lost more than 1 per cent of its previous total. The two big parties suffered disproportionately in one particular respect: amid allegations of vote-rigging by Sinn Féin, the

SDLP lost its long-standing control of Derry City Council; and the UUP lost out in four other councils, becoming a minority in Belfast, in County Fermanagh and in two small towns, Cookstown and Strabane. There is an expectation in some quarters that Sinn Féin and the DUP will improve their position in the 2001 local government contest; it is certainly true that both parties are devoting much effort and resources to doing just that.

The district councils were for long the only forums in which locally elected politicians regularly confronted each other; so despite the councils' limited powers they were a focus for political controversy. Debates on issues outside their strict remit were a regular feature, playing out much of Northern Ireland's day-to-day political drama. To take just one example, the growing presence of Sinn Féin councillors – until the mid-1990s as full-hearted supporters of the IRA's armed struggle – provoked much disruption of council business by unionist members in the late 1980s and early 1990s. On the other hand, some non-unionist (in effect SDLP) controlled councils have adopted a policy of 'power-sharing', which usually takes the form of a rotation of senior offices, such as mayor/council leader and committee chairs. This has had the effect of improving inter-party relations, and avoiding the bitterness that characterises the conduct of business on other councils.

Settling an ancient quarrel

There were several major pushes by the British government in the 1970s and '80s to persuade the parties in Northern Ireland to reach some kind of accord on a resolution of the conflict. Although one of these, the Sunningdale Agreement, did produce a short-lived restoration of devolution to a multi-party government in 1974 (which is referred to further below), little success attended the government's efforts. However, the first major move in the process that culminated in the 1998 Good Friday Agreement was taken in the Republic, when the 'New Ireland Forum' met in Dublin in 1983. The Forum was composed of representatives of all but three of the main political parties on the island (the UUP and DUP refused to attend, and Sinn Féin was excluded because of its support for violence). For many years, the basic assumption of Irish nationalists had been that a united Ireland was the only possible solution to the Northern Ireland problem. However, the Forum Report, published in May 1984, set out all the options that ought to be open for discussion. These included the traditional 'unitary' Irish state – although few observers saw this as a realistic possibility. More interestingly, the Report outlined proposals for joint authority over Northern Ireland by Britain and the Republic, and for forms of a federal or confederal state. Although Margaret Thatcher, on behalf of the UK government, dismissed all of the Forum's main options rather peremptorily soon after their publication, they served as an opening agenda for serious discussion later on.

First fruit was the Anglo-Irish Agreement of November 1985, which, as already noted, gave the Irish government an entitlement to be consulted about a wide range of Northern Ireland's internal affairs. While diehard nationalists were angered at the associated formal recognition by Dublin of Northern Ireland's status within the UK, moderate nationalist opinion was strongly in favour: after more than sixty years, what was always viewed as a unionist veto on progress had effectively been removed. Unionists, for their part, were shocked and dismayed at the involvement of the 'foreign' Irish government in the internal affairs of Northern Ireland. Their anger eventually led to street protests, strikes and civil disobedience.

Progress thereafter was painfully slow, and it was not until April 1991 that the first attempt at talks involving all Northern Ireland politicians (except Sinn Féin) and the British and Irish governments got off the ground. Although they ended without agreement, there was general acceptance of the analysis of John Hume, leader of the SDLP. He had been arguing for some time that there were 'three strands' to be attended to if progress was to be made in creating a new future: one 'internal' to Northern Ireland; one to do with North–South relationships; and one covering the conduct of relations between Britain and the Irish Republic.

In the meantime, Sinn Féin was engaged in a major rethink of its position. From the early 1980s onwards there had been a conscious turn to politics by the republican movement, and the approach to begin with was neatly captured by a senior Sinn Féin figure in a notorious conference speech in 1985; he said that the movement was going forward 'with a ballot box in one hand and an Armalite [automatic rifle] in the other'. That a major change had taken place was marked most signally by the reopening of previously inconclusive talks with the SDLP in the early 1990s. Though most observers expected little to come of this dialogue, Hume and Gerry Adams (an important member of the leadership of Sinn Féin) did eventually arrive at a common position. This was put directly to the Irish government, and was said to be the major influence on a statement by the Minister for Foreign Affairs, in October 1993, of six democratic principles upon which he considered a settlement in Northern Ireland ought to be based:

- The people of Ireland, north and south, should freely determine their future.
- This could be expressed in new structures arising out of the three-stranded relationship.
- There could be no change in Northern Ireland's status without freely given majority consent.
- This consent could legitimately be withheld.
- The consent principle should be written into the Irish Constitution.
- And a place should be found at the negotiating table for Sinn Féin, once the IRA had renounced violence.

Next, incorporating virtually all of this, came the Downing Street Declaration of December 1993, signed by the British Prime Minister and the Taoiseach. It also spelled out for the third time in as many years that the British government had no 'selfish strategic or economic interest in Northern Ireland'. The object of this declaration was to assist Sinn Féin in persuading the IRA that there was no longer, if there ever had been, any justification for the use of other than democratic methods in pursuit of republican political aims. It took until 31 August 1994 for the IRA to be convinced and to call a cease-fire; but even then the IRA refused to declare categorically that the cease-fire was permanent. Soon after, the UVF and UDA also announced cease-fires, conditional upon the maintenance of that of the IRA.

The most important effect (after some hesitation on the part of the British government about the permanence of the cessation of violence) was to bring Sinn Féin, the PUP and UDP into direct contact with the British and Irish governments for the first time. Sinn Féin and the loyalists also took part in a new 'Forum for Peace and Reconciliation' set up by the Irish government, intended to promote 'agreement and trust between both traditions in Ireland'. British and Irish radio and television broadcasting bans on paramilitaries and their political associates had also been lifted by this stage, giving leading Sinn Féin figures like Adams access to the public airwaves for the first time for many years.

Support from abroad, especially from the United States, for what was now being called the 'peace process' was soon forthcoming. British troops were off the streets for the first time for almost a quarter of a century. And in February 1995 the British and Irish governments issued their 'Framework' documents setting out the parameters within which all-party negotiations might take place.

Decommissioning emerges as a barrier to progress

The issue of the disposal or decommissioning of paramilitary weapons proved to be a major stumbling block to the peace process – and has remained to bedevil it ever since. The polar positions were, on the one side, that Sinn Féin, the UDP and the PUP could not possibly take part in talks so long as their paramilitary associates continued to hold arms – and could thus return to violence if they were not satisfied with the progress being made or did not approve of the outcome of negotiations. On the other side, the IRA, UVF and UDA simply refused to countenance any suggestion of a surrender of weapons until negotiations were complete.

In an effort to resolve the impasse, a small team headed by former US Senator George Mitchell (whose services were volunteered by his friend President Clinton) was invited to rule on the question. The 'Mitchell Principles' incorporated a compromise on the weapons issue, by proposing

that 'decommissioning talks' run in parallel with the substantive negotiations. The British government was not immediately seized of the value of
this and, in what was claimed by some to be a deliberate diversion, accepted a
Unionist demand that there be an election for membership of a 'Peace Forum'
(the results are reported above), from which the negotiating teams for the
main talks would also be selected. Sinn Féin and the SDLP saw no need for an
election and were frustrated by what they viewed as another British delaying
tactic.

The significance of the IRA's refusal to declare its 1994 cease-fire permanent became all too apparent when a bomb exploded at Canary Wharf in
London in February 1996, killing two people who had nothing whatever to
do with the conflict in Northern Ireland. This was followed by several other
IRA actions against so-called economic targets in Britain, as well as a mortar
assault on a British army base in Germany. The justification offered by the
IRA for these attacks was British and Unionist insincerity and prevarication,
and the failure to set a date for the commencement of all-party talks.

Sinn Féin refused to condemn the IRA's resumption of violence and was
immediately excluded from further contacts with ministers of both governments. In the hope of achieving a restoration of the IRA cease-fire, however,
London and Dublin agreed to set the opening of all-party negotiations for 10
June 1996. But this was not sufficient to convince the IRA that the talks
would be productive; and Sinn Féin was refused entry despite its assertion
that this was a denial of the new mandate that its increased vote in the Peace
Forum election had demonstrated.

More marching and more guns[11]

The resumption of IRA violence, which took up most press attention between
March and mid-summer, was briefly superseded in its news value by the
opening of the 1996 'marching season'. Plainly against the wishes of the
inhabitants, two important parades by the Orange Order were forced through
Catholic areas and, in the worst communal violence for many years, widespread rioting and arson took place in both republican and loyalist areas.
Although some compromises on the routing of parades were later reached,
the government was persuaded to set up an independent commission to rule
on whether particular parades and demonstrations should be permitted.
Given an impossible task, it is hardly surprising that the Parades Commission
has since met with little success.

The cease-fires of the two main unionist/loyalist paramilitary groups
remained theoretically intact during the same period; but in practice there
was the adoption of a 'no claim/no blame' stratagem, which essentially
meant that no admission of involvement in a number of significant incidents
was made, even though it was fairly clear who had been responsible for each

of them. By contrast, IRA actions continued, with full responsibility being acknowledged. They included the planting of a massive car bomb in June in the commercial heart of the city of Manchester in England; an attack in October on the British army's Northern Ireland headquarters in Lisburn, County Antrim; bomb threats which caused the postponement of the annual Grand National horse race at Aintree (near Liverpool) in April 1997; and the shooting dead of two members of the RUC in Lurgan, County Armagh, in June 1997. In face of all this there was little confidence that Sinn Féin would be able to persuade the IRA to resume its cease-fire. As a result, the all-party talks that flowed from the Forum elections, and by which Sinn Féin had set much store, proceeded without its participation. However, it is of some significance that the talks were to be chaired by Senator Mitchell, the outcome of whose earlier efforts had been so widely admired.

Sinn Féin re-enters negotiations – with new thinking

The Labour Party, led by Tony Blair, won a resounding victory in the British general election of May 1997. With the full support of the Irish government, Blair moved quickly; and despite the IRA having resumed its campaign of violence, he authorised the opening of lines of communication between civil servants and Sinn Féin. The shooting of the policemen in Lurgan caused these contacts to be broken off, but the unexpected reinstatement of the IRA cease-fire in late July – and a five-week period during which the new Labour Secretary of State for Northern Ireland, Dr Marjorie ('Mo') Mowlam, was satisfied that it was being observed – was quickly followed in September by Sinn Féin's signing up to the Mitchell Principles and the entry of its representatives to the talks.

It is impossible to offer a confident interpretation of the approach of the republican movement at that point, for two main reasons: first, there was the inevitable secrecy surrounding the activity of the IRA; and second, the public witnessed the quite remarkable adherence to whatever was the current 'party line' by every single spokesperson for Sinn Féin. Hard-bitten journalists were in awe of the degree to which they all 'sang from the same hymn-sheet'. It is clear, nevertheless, that profound revisions of previous Sinn Féin positions had taken place. By entering political negotiations involving the British government that were essentially premised upon Northern Ireland remaining part of the UK, Sinn Féin was departing from what many would have regarded as a key tenet of the republican ideological tradition. Another significant departure from the canon arose from acceptance of the Mitchell Principles, since these obviously entailed a rejection of the legitimacy of 'armed struggle' in pursuit of the republican objective of a united Ireland. Arguably just as important a transformation was the implicit acknowledgement that the British had no 'imperialistic' reasons for remaining in Northern Ireland.

It goes without saying that Sinn Féin's unionist enemies – in their various party guises – remained suspicious of these apparent changes of heart. The leader of the UUP was prepared nevertheless to set his reservations aside, at least temporarily, in order to join the talks process. However, while concluding that at least some progress was possible through dialogue, the Ulster Unionists were indignant at the failure of any of the paramilitary groups to begin to decommission their weapons. They thus had major misgivings about either themselves or the British government dealing directly with the political representatives of these groups – and in particular with representatives of what the UUP insisted on calling 'Sinn Féin/IRA'. As a result the Ulster Unionists had to 'swallow hard' at several points in the negotiations. But even the first meeting since 1921 between a British Prime Minister and Sinn Féin representatives, which took place at government buildings at Stormont in mid-October (following which Blair was mobbed by an angry unionist crowd in a Belfast shopping centre), did not shake the UUP's determination to remain in the talks. Its response was the same to a further meeting between Blair and the Adams/McGuinness team behind the hallowed doors of 10 Downing Street itself in December, which many unionist-minded people regarded as a traitorous act by the Prime Minister of the UK.

What of the other parties elected to the 1996 Forum? The DUP and the tiny UKUP decided at an early stage that they were not prepared to engage in negotiations that included surrogates for paramilitary groups. Their contribution was thus confined to barracking from the margins. The SDLP, it goes without saying, was involved wholeheartedly, having worked towards the setting up of serious all-party talks for the best part of a quarter of a century. Committed unquestionably to the success of the new process, the SDLP's approach was as much that of honest broker as of partisan. The Alliance Party was of a similar mind.

Dedicated to the success of the talks, and thus constructive in approach also, were the PUP and UDP. Both made special efforts to support the position of David Trimble, leader of the Ulster Unionists, as against that of his many nay-saying colleagues in the UUP. Finally, from among the minor parties represented in the talks, the Women's Coalition should be picked out as having had a disproportionately beneficent effect on the attitudes of its fellow negotiators. Yet despite all this apparent goodwill, the process made so little progress that by Christmas 1998 the parties had failed even to agree a list of issues to be discussed.

The violence goes on

Meanwhile, in the background, violence continued. In early December 1998 a Catholic man was murdered as he left a sports club in the northern outskirts of Belfast. Three days after Christmas, Billy Wright, leader of the Loyalist Volunteer Force (LVF) – an anti-talks breakaway from the UVF – was shot dead in prison by inmates from the Irish National Liberation Army (INLA), a republican splinter group that had not declared a cease-fire. The reaction was completely predictable: within a month, seven Catholics and one Protestant were dead. And while much of the blame was laid at the door of the LVF, there were strong suspicions that mainstream loyalists, ostensibly on cease-fire, were involved in at least some of these deaths. Then, in late January 1999, another IRA splinter group, the 'Continuity' IRA (CIRA), exploded a bomb outside a nightclub in Enniskillen, County Fermanagh.

The RUC Chief Constable (the head of the RUC) ventured that the Ulster Freedom Fighters (UFF) – a cover name for the UDA, which was represented at the talks by the UDP – were indeed involved in some of the December and January killings. The UFF admitted this was so on the day after the RUC announcement and at the end of January the UDP was forced to leave the talks until the Secretary of State was satisfied that the UDA/UFF had resumed cease-fire. Then it was Sinn Féin's turn. For a time, 'punishment beatings' of persons thought to be minor criminals were the only obvious evidence of continued republican violence. But in early February a man said to be an illicit drugs dealer was shot dead in Dunmurry, south of Belfast, by an IRA front organisation known as 'Direct Action Against Drugs'. Next day, in the same area, a furniture shop owner who had UDA connections was also killed. A week later, and about fifteen miles away, a Catholic man was murdered in what had all the appearance of an IRA execution. The Chief Constable offered the further opinion that each of these killings had indeed involved the IRA; so Sinn Féin too was expelled from the talks for a period.

In the meantime the CIRA appeared to have been responsible for several actions: car bombs in Moira, County Down, and Portadown, County Armagh, in February; a further car bomb clearly intended for a Northern Ireland town which was intercepted by the police in Dundalk in the Irish Republic in March; and mortar attacks on police stations in Armagh City and Forkhill, County Armagh, also in March. That wicked month also witnessed several other acts of violence. There was the murder by the LVF of two friends, one a Protestant and one a Catholic, in a pub in Poyntzpass, County Down. Then one of those suspected of the murder was himself killed by fellow inmates in the Maze Prison – amid rumours that he was an RUC informer. No one was charged with his killing, which had been set up to look like suicide. Towards the end of March the INLA was responsible for the shooting dead of a former RUC officer in Armagh; and Gardaí intercepted a further massive CIRA car bomb on its way to Britain at a ferry port in the Republic.

Slow progress at the talks

In January 1999, in an effort to move things forward a bit, the British and Irish governments put forward their own joint proposals for a settlement.

entitled Heads of Agreement. Almost immediately Sinn Féin demanded and got another meeting with Blair in London, at which it protested at the 'unionist bias' of the document. The IRA reinforced the Sinn Féin stand by issuing a statement pronouncing the Heads of Agreement an unacceptable basis for any move forward. The talks moved from Belfast to London and Dublin for short periods with the purpose of increasing the freedom of movement of the negotiators – by taking them away from the day-to-day pressures at home. But despite this, and the return of the UDP and Sinn Féin to the process, progress was slow.

So on 26 March the talks chairman, Senator Mitchell, set a deadline for agreement of 9 April. This moved the process on a little, but with only three days to go, and no conclusion in sight, Mitchell was obliged to put forward his own draft agreement for consideration by the parties. This time it was the Ulster Unionists who were upset – at what they felt was much 'too nationalist' a document. Jolted by this, Prime Minister Blair flew to Belfast to put his own reputation on the line in the search for a settlement. The main negotiators for the two governments had until then been Mo Mowlam and David Andrews, the Irish Foreign Minister. However, Taoiseach Bertie Ahern also became engaged – even though this meant taking only a short break from the talks to attend his mother's funeral. As it was, the 9 April deadline came – and went; but the final agreement was actually reached the very next day, Good Friday.

The Good Friday Agreement

The Belfast or 'Good Friday' Agreement is intended to end thirty years of violence and strife. Its provisions can be categorised under a number of headings.[12]

Constitutional issues

On fundamental constitutional questions, the most important aspect of the Agreement is the 'principle of consent' – in other words that change in the status of Northern Ireland as part of the UK can take place only with the consent of a majority of its people. If the situation *does* arise where a majority wants change, both governments will be obliged to give full effect to whatever it is the people want. Agreed legislative changes include:

- repeal of the Government of Ireland Act 1920 – which claims British jurisdiction over the whole of the island of Ireland;
- provision for polls to be taken of the people of Northern Ireland, seeking their opinion on the constitutional status, which must be at least seven years apart;
- a referendum of the people of the Republic seeking their endorsement of the Agreement itself, the amendment of Articles 2 and 3 of Bunreacht na

hÉireann (to remove the 'territorial claim' over Northern Ireland), and the creation of the North–South bodies (on which see more below).

Plainly, the key changes here are the reassurance to unionists flowing from the elimination of the Republic's constitutional claim to jurisdiction over Northern Ireland and the general acceptance of the consent principle.

Strand One

In respect of structures within Northern Ireland itself, described as Strand One provisions, the following were agreed:

- the creation of a 108-member Assembly elected by STV;
- 'key' decisions of the Assembly to be taken on a cross-community basis;
- members to register themselves as 'unionist', 'nationalist' or 'other';
- for a decision to be made by simple majority, there must be a majority in favour among both unionist and nationalist assembly members; alternatively, a decision can be made with just 40 per cent of unionist or nationalist votes, but only if there is an overall 60 per cent support of the total members voting;
- 'key' decisions include the election of the Assembly Chairperson, the First Minister and his or her Deputy, confirmation of standing orders for the conduct of Assembly business, and budget allocations;
- committees with a policy development, scrutiny and advisory role to 'shadow' ministers in the conduct of their duties;
- an Executive Authority (or Cabinet) to be made up of the First Minister, the Deputy First Minister and ten other ministers with specific departmental responsibilities; ministerial posts, committee chairs and committee places to be allocated in proportion to party strengths;
- the Assembly to be required to deal with legislation in areas specifically devolved to it by Westminster, but on matters normally reserved to the Secretary of State for Northern Ireland only with his or her approval.

On the basis of all this, it is clear that a wide coalition of parties will always take part in government. It is also clear that each 'side' will have a veto, which can be exercised in a variety of ways.

Strand Two

Under Strand Two, which is concerned with Northern Ireland's relationship with the Republic of Ireland, the following points were agreed:

- the creation of a North–South Council to bring together ministers to 'develop consultation, cooperation and action ... on matters of mutual interest';
- a joint Council Secretariat made up of civil servants from both sides of the border to support the Council in its work;

- decisions to be made by agreement between ministers from Northern Ireland and the Republic, who will be responsible, as appropriate, to the Oireachtas or to the Assembly;
- to prevent any boycotting of the North–South Council, participation to be 'an essential responsibility attaching to relevant posts in the two administrations'.
- the Council to have one plenary meeting each year, involving the First Minister, his or her Deputy and the Taoiseach, but relevant ministers to have bilateral meetings 'on a regular and frequent basis'.

The main thrust of the measures agreed under Strand Two is to meet nationalist aspirations as regards the engagement of the government of the Republic in Northern Ireland affairs. This was a hard-fought part of the Agreement, with unionists attempting to minimise the involvement of the Irish government and nationalists seeking to maximise it. Balance of a kind was achieved by giving the North–South Council real powers (as demanded by nationalists) but restricting quite severely the areas in which it is to have an element of jurisdiction (a negotiating objective of the unionists).

Strand Three

Strand Three was intended to deal with 'East/West' relations:

- it required the creation of a British–Irish Council, made up of representatives of the two sovereign governments, together with those representing devolved institutions in Northern Ireland, Scotland, Wales, the Channel Islands and the Isle of Man;
- the Council is intended to 'exchange information, discuss, consult and use best endeavours to reach agreement on cooperation on matters of mutual interest';
- suitable subjects for discussion are suggested in the Agreement – transport, agriculture, the environment, culture, health and education, as well as joint approaches on subjects of common interest at an EU level;
- the British–Irish Council can agree on common actions and policy, but participants can opt not to participate in these.

Strand Three is thus intended mainly to support unionist commitment to an older, common 'British Isles' heritage.

The social justice agenda

Changes proposed in the Agreement, most of which have been implemented, included the following:

- the European Convention on Human Rights to be incorporated into law in both Northern Ireland and the Republic;

- a new all-embracing Northern Ireland Equality Commission to be formed out of the existing Fair Employment Commission, the Equal Opportunities Commission, the Commission for Racial Equality and the Northern Ireland Disability Council;
- the government of the Republic to bring its own equality provisions into line with those in Northern Ireland (to this end it has already established a Human Rights Commission of its own, and this will enter into a Joint Committee with the equivalent Northern Ireland body);
- the Irish government is also required to ratify the Council of Europe Convention on National Minorities and to implement 'enhanced' employment equality law;
- the British government is obliged to produce a new economic development strategy for Northern Ireland and to ensure fair distribution of the fruits of such a plan;
- finally, there is recognition of the need to respect the Irish and Ulster-Scots languages, as well as the languages of the various ethnic groups in Northern Ireland.

Of particular interest here is the reciprocal commitment by the government of the Republic to bring its own policies and procedures into line with those in Northern Ireland.

Guns, bombs, policing and criminal justice

Because they followed on almost inevitably from the cessation of paramilitary activity, among the least problematic of the sections of the Agreement under this general heading seemed to be the undertakings by the British government to reduce the numbers of troops in Northern Ireland, to dismantle security installations and to repeal emergency powers legislation. However, in early 2001 the removal of army posts along the border came into unexpected contention – on which see more below. The acceptance by the Irish government in the Agreement that it must dismantle the fairly draconian Offences Against the State Act, introduced specifically to deal with security crises associated with the Northern Ireland troubles, is another interesting piece of reciprocation.

As we have already had reason to note, the decommissioning of the arsenal of weapons in the hands of the various paramilitary groupings was always going to be one of the most difficult issues in the talks. For the Ulster Unionists the decommissioning of illegal weapons was mooted as a precondition for virtually every move forward in the peace process, but each time they gave ground. On the other hand, the politicians involved in the talks who had links to paramilitary groups adamantly refused to enter into any specific commitments – certainly no immediate ones – on this score. The result was the section of the final Agreement dealing with decommissioning, which is a manifest fudge:

- All parties reaffirmed their *commitment to total disarmament* and confirmed their intention *to work constructively* with the Independent Commission on Decommissioning (set up before the Agreement, and further discussed below).
- The parties also agreed to *use their influence* to achieve decommissioning *within two years* of the endorsement of the Agreement by the electorates of Northern Ireland and the Republic.

Since the wording of this section has come to assume considerable import-ance in the period since the conclusion of the Agreement, it is worth noting in particular the words italicised, which are directly quoted from it.

On policing, the outcome was also somewhat blurred. On the one hand, Sinn Féin was demanding the disbandment of the RUC, claiming that it was a discredited, sectarian force. On the other, the Ulster Unionists were deter-mined to ensure that the RUC, which had 'held the line' against terrorism for thirty years and more, should not become a 'victim of compromise'. The outcome was agreement that an independent commission be appointed 'to make recommendations for future policing arrangements in Northern Ireland'. Chris Patten, the last British Governor of Hong Kong before the territory was restored to China, and who had also served as a junior minister in the NIO, was eventually appointed as chair of the Policing Commission.

After the issue of decommissioning, arguably the most controversial part of the Agreement was that both governments would 'put in place mechan-isms for the accelerated release of paramilitary prisoners'. It was this that led to the walkout of a trusted aide of the UUP leader during the very last hours of the Agreement negotiations. Essentially the argument is that this provision showed no thought for the victims of violence and their relatives. However, what it was essentially about was keeping the erstwhile, 'reformed' para-militaries on board, and tying the IRA, the UDA and the UVF – hopefully irreversibly – into democracy.

It is worthy of note that despite the anger of some people at the release of murderers and bombers, there is no doubt that many of Northern Ireland's citizens – on both sides of the divide – accept the claim that the majority of those imprisoned for paramilitary crimes would never have become offenders in a 'normal' society. So while they may be unhappy at the releases, which had been completed by late 2000, they understand that there would have been no Agreement without them.

Sunningdale mark II?

We might finally seek to compare the Good Friday Agreement with the Sunningdale Agreement, which led to the power-sharing Executive of 1974. It was negotiated, following elections for a Northern Ireland Assembly, by the British and Irish governments together with representatives of the SDLP, the UUP and the Alliance Party. Unfortunately, the Executive collapsed after just a few months, for two main reasons. First, the IRA was convinced that the prorogation of the Northern Ireland Parliament in 1972 had been a direct consequence of its armed campaign and viewed this as but the first sign of a crumbling of British will to 'remain' in Northern Ireland. The theory, therefore, was that 'one last heave' would send the British home – thus the maintenance of the bombing campaign. Second, there had been strong loyalist opposition from the beginning to the Agreement. Against the background of continuing IRA violence, and a weak response to the setting up of illegal UDA-manned roadblocks by the Secretary of State, a loyalist anti-Sunningdale work stoppage spread to the point where essential utilities such as power and water supplies were threatened. The Unionist members of the Executive had little choice but to resign.

This ought not, however, to distract us from the significance of the main components of the Sunningdale Agreement, which in broad terms included the following:

• acceptance by all parties, including the Irish government and the SDLP, that the constitutional status of Northern Ireland could not be changed without the consent of a majority;
• acknowledgement by all parties, including the British government and the UUP, that there was an 'Irish dimension' to the Northern Ireland problem;
• acceptance that a Northern Ireland Executive drawn from members of the Assembly should be made up of as wide a voluntary coalition of parties as possible, based on party strength;
• acceptance that the Irish dimension should be given expression through the creation of the Council of Ireland.

There is plainly much more detail, and much more compulsion, in the Good Friday Agreement, but many people have identified warmly with the sentiment expressed in the withering words credited to the SDLP's Seamus Mallon: that the Good Friday Agreement was just 'Sunningdale for slow learners'.

Making a new start?

There was palpable euphoria in the weeks following the conclusion of the Good Friday Agreement, and the people of Northern Ireland and the Republic of Ireland duly endorsed it – though with varying degrees of enthusiasm. In Northern Ireland only a narrow majority of unionist-minded people gave it their approval; but an overwhelming nationalist thumbs-up ensured that it received the psychologically key 70 per cent breakthrough that was generally felt to be necessary for success. In the Republic the endorsement was universal, wholehearted and almost unequivocal.

The Assembly elections that followed produced almost exactly the same result as the Agreement referendum, in terms of the broad pro- and anti- vote.

David Trimble was appointed First Minister Designate and John Hume stood aside to permit his colleague Seamus Mallon to become Deputy First Minister Designate. Then everything ground to a halt, as old preoccupations reasserted themselves. The rejection by the nationalist residents of the Garvaghy Road in Portadown, County Armagh, of efforts to persuade them to permit the passage of a traditional Orange Order march back from a religious service in the Church of Ireland parish church at Drumcree produced the third stand-off in as many years. The judgement of the Parades Commission was in favour of the local residents. But a substantial confrontation between Orangemen and their supporters and the RUC ended only after a petrol bomb thrown into a house in Ballymoney, County Antrim, caused the death of three children of a mixed Catholic/Protestant relationship.

But greater tragedy was to follow. On 15 August 1998, a bomb left in the market town of Omagh, County Tyrone, by a new breakaway group describing itself as the 'Real' IRA (RIRA), killed twenty-eight people; another victim died in hospital some weeks later. It was the worst single incident in all the troubles in Northern Ireland. And most notably, it provoked calls from various sections of the republican movement for the violence to be called off once and for all. The Irish Republican Socialist Party (IRSP), the political wing of the INLA, insisted that the armed struggle could no longer be justified. Adams, in his capacity as President of Sinn Féin, announced that 'the violence we have seen must be for all of us now a thing of the past – over, done with and gone'. And even the RIRA itself said that it believed that a continuation of its campaign was futile 'in the circumstances of Omagh and the Mitchell [Principles] agreement'.

Although the two governments were committed by the Agreement to the repeal of various emergency powers, their first reaction was to introduce new anti-terrorist legislation. That the Omagh bombing was a real and heart-rending watershed was symbolised by visits to the small town by Tony Blair on 26 August, and by Bill Clinton, on his second visit to Northern Ireland, on 3 September 1998.

Subtleties and complexities

In order to understand the complexities of the situation, it is worth dwelling in some detail on what happened between August 1998 and the end of 1999; for that August marked the beginning of a standoff which was to last longer than anyone could possibly have imagined. In a leaked document the UUP was reported as saying there would be 'no chance' of an Executive being formed under the Good Friday Agreement without some decommissioning of IRA weapons. On this stance, incidentally, the UUP had the specific support of John Bruton, the leader of Fine Gael, the second largest party in the Republic. The IRA and Sinn Féin, on the other hand, responded by claiming that there was nothing in the Good Friday Agreement that prevented the immediate establishment of an Executive, including Sinn Féin members, whether or not there was decommissioning by the IRA. More importantly, Sinn Féin was also beginning to say loudly and clearly that it simply could not deliver decommissioning *before* an Executive was formed. The SDLP, for its part, acknowledged that the wording of the Agreement meant that there was no precondition to Sinn Féin's entry into an Executive, but nevertheless called on the IRA to make a confidence-building decommissioning gesture.

Meanwhile, the process of opening the gates of the jails began with the release on 11 September 1998 of the first seven paramilitary prisoners. Within a fortnight the RUC Chief Constable reported to the press that a number of British army installations and check-points were to be demolished forthwith. The announcement that the Nobel Prize for Peace would be awarded jointly to John Hume and David Trimble distracted attention from the decommissioning row, but only briefly. Hardly surprisingly, the Agreement deadline of 31 October for the formation of the Executive, of the Northern Ireland Assembly and of the North–South Council was missed. Of arguably great significance was that during the SDLP annual conference in November, Mallon indicated that his party would help to remove Sinn Féin from the Executive if the IRA failed to decommission within the specified timescale. He added, however, that the SDLP would not support any attempt by Unionists to 'rewrite' the Good Friday Agreement.

But numerous comings and goings between London, Belfast and Dublin by Prime Minister Blair, Taoiseach Bertie Ahern and the leaders of the pro-Agreement parties over the next couple of months produced no progress whatever. In what some regarded as a thinly veiled threat, the IRA's New Year message for 1999 said that the Good Friday Agreement had failed to deliver meaningful change and that Unionists were pursuing conditions 'that had contributed to the breakdown of the 1994 cease-fire'. Although it had earlier been reported that a General Army Convention of the IRA in December had decided that there would not be any decommissioning, the New Year message did come as a surprise to many people, because it revealed as clearly as could be that the IRA did not feel in any way bound by the decommissioning section of the Agreement – even though its republican colleagues in Sinn Féin had signed up to it. This inevitably fuelled pro-Agreement unionist fears that they had been drawn into a trap, the main worry being that the IRA was going to feel free to break its second cease-fire if things did not go the way it wished. Recognising this fear, Mallon called on the IRA to state unequivocally that its campaign of violence was over – to no avail.

In mid-March things seemed to move on a little. A joint statement by Blair, Ahern and President Clinton urged the leaders of the parties in Northern Ireland to meet a new deadline of 2 April 1999 for full implementation of the Good Friday Agreement. All-party talks, including the Prime Minister and the Taoiseach, began again at Hillsborough Castle, County Down, the official residence of the Secretary of State, on 29 March. A few participants in the talks reported some progress; but this seemed to rely on a generous reading of the IRA's annual Easter statement – which contained the rather anodyne claim that the IRA 'wholeheartedly support[ed] efforts to secure a lasting resolution to the conflict'. The talks seemed to end on an upbeat note, with a document entitled the Hillsborough Declaration. It set out a 'framework for progress' towards establishing the Executive – and a new deadline for it to be set up in three weeks. Within few days, however, a Sinn Féin spokesperson issued a formal statement claiming that the Hillsborough Declaration departed from the Good Friday Agreement and was thus unacceptable.

Another deadline

The rounds of discussions thus dragged on in both London and Belfast, but had made so little progress by mid-May that Blair tried an overused tactic: he declared an 'absolute' deadline of 30 June 1999 for the formation of an Executive and the devolution of power to the Assembly. This decision was finally provoked by the failure of UUP Assembly members to give their approval to proposals thought to have been agreed by Trimble with the Irish government, the SDLP and Sinn Féin. These would have seen the appointment of ministers to an Executive triggered within a week or so, and full devolution by the end of June, following a report on 'progress' on decommissioning by General John de Chastelain, head of the Independent Commission on Decommissioning. The retired Canadian General had been a member of the group that produced the Mitchell Principles, and the Commission was created in what turned out to be an unsuccessful attempt to take decommissioning off the negotiating table.

With only just over a week to go to Blair's deadline, Trimble invited his anti-Agreement colleague Jeffrey Donaldson to rejoin the UUP talks team. This immediately dispelled hopes that the UUP might be persuaded to proceed with a less than hard-and-fast agreement on IRA decommissioning. By this time the Taoiseach was making no secret of the Irish government's view that the Northern Ireland Executive was going to have to be up and running *before* any weapons were likely to be decommissioned – because paramilitaries would disarm only 'in the context of a confidence in functioning democratic institutions'. But while Blair claimed that 'seismic shifts' in Northern Ireland's political landscape had resulted from the talks, his 'absolute deadline' passed without the establishment of the Executive.

So as not to lose momentum entirely, the two governments quickly issued a document called *The Way Forward*, which outlined a procedure by which the Northern Ireland Executive would be set up and arms would be decommissioned – amid hints that the IRA was preparing to engage, however remotely, with the de Chastelain Commission. Trimble, in the meantime, said that the Ulster Unionists would not reject *The Way Forward* without consideration, but that they would require 'further reassurances'. However, picking up on an earlier remark by Gerry Adams, he stated the UUP's clear willingness to 'jump together' with Sinn Féin in forming an Executive because, he said, there was no resistance within his Assembly party to setting up an Executive fully inclusive of all parties – provided there was decommissioning.

Twisting Trimble's arm

Evidence that he was actually being pushed into a corner by his anti-Agreement colleagues came when a prearranged effort was made on 15 July 1999 to form the Executive: Trimble and his fellow UUP members simply failed to turn up for the appointed sitting of the Assembly. In the event, an Executive made up of SDLP and Sinn Féin members was formed, but was disbanded almost immediately because it failed to meet the unionist/nationalist cross-community support demanded by the Good Friday Agreement. In obvious frustration, and insulted by the behaviour of the UUP, Mallon tendered his resignation as Deputy First Minister designate.

Within a few days, the UUP claimed vindication of its stand on the decommissioning question following confirmation from security sources, first, that the IRA was responsible for the death of a taxi driver, Charles Bennett, and, second, that a Florida-based gun-smuggling operation had been uncovered which bore all the marks of IRA involvement. According to some newspaper reports, republican sources claimed Bennett was killed to pacify hardliners over decommissioning and the lack of political progress. There was also unofficial acknowledgement (subsequently confirmed in consequence of a legal action in the United States) that the attempt to import high-powered weapons by post from Florida was indeed an IRA operation. In late August, Mo Mowlam, whose decision in these matters was final under the Agreement, said she had no doubt the IRA was involved in both the Bennett murder and the Florida gun-running but, to the consternation of some, she ruled that the IRA cease-fire had not broken down.

Meanwhile, in search of a mechanism to advance matters, and against a background of street violence associated with various parades, Blair called for a formal review of the Good Friday Agreement – something provided for in its own terms. The ever-genial Senator Mitchell was prevailed upon to return from the United States once more to act as chair. Although he made clear that the focus would be on the issue of decommissioning and its relationship to the formation of an Executive, the discussions had no sooner started, on 6 September, than a major complicating ingredient was added to the mix. The Patten Commission produced its report on the future of policing in Northern Ireland.

It recommended a radical overhaul, covering police structure, training, ethos, symbols and composition. While the RUC was accepted as the basis upon which a new service would be built, the report concentrated on the need for much stronger representation of Catholics in its ranks, the disbandment of some controversial units within the existing force and changes to the RUC name and badge. Almost the only major party to have a good word for the Patten report, the SDLP indicated that it provided a sound basis for progress. Since it fell far short of recommending disbandment of the RUC, Sinn Féin could hardly welcome the document, but its response was not entirely negative. However, Trimble was totally scathing. Offended in particular by the proposed renaming, and the casting off of the RUC's symbols, he described the report as 'the most shoddy piece of work I have seen in my entire life'. At a UUP conference a month later he succeeded in killing off an attempt by anti-Agreement members to tie his negotiating hands at the Mitchell review. But there then began an unfortunate linking of policing reform and decommissioning, when the conference unanimously approved a motion dismissing the Patten report as a threat to Northern Ireland's security so long as arms remained in the hands of the paramilitaries.

Trimble had something to cheer about later, in October, when Peter Mandelson, someone whose name he had suggested to the Prime Minister as being less nationalist leaning, replaced Mowlam as Secretary of State for Northern Ireland in a Cabinet reshuffle. In the meantime, the Mitchell review became less a review than an extended new negotiating session on the decommissioning question. Mallon, plainly fed up, described the arguments between Sinn Féin and the UUP on the question as a 'miserable dispute'.

Confidence building?

What started to emerge as a possible route out of the misery was a carefully choreographed set of 'confidence building steps'. In the end the procedure adopted was as follows:

- On 16 November 1999, simultaneous statements were issued by Adams and Trimble, committing themselves to the full implementation of the Good Friday Agreement; and while Trimble recognised the legitimate aspirations of nationalists to a united Ireland, Adams spoke of working with, not against, the Ulster Unionists in the future.
- All the other pro-Agreement parties then issued statements reiterating their endorsement of it.
- Next day the IRA released a statement saying it was committed to a lasting peace and that it believed the Agreement would contribute to that. The IRA also endorsed the leadership of Sinn Féin in all the negotiations that had taken place.
- More importantly, the IRA agreed, as a gesture of good faith, to nominate an interlocutor to enter discussions on decommissioning with the de Chastelain Commission.

- This enabled Senator Mitchell to issue a report on the review, which concluded that the basis now existed for devolution to occur and for an Executive to be formed.
- It also enabled Trimble to go to a meeting of the ruling Ulster Unionist Council of his Party with a recommendation for acceptance of the deal. He emphasised that the entry of the UUP into government with Sinn Féin could be time limited, so as to ensure that decommissioning would follow devolution. His proposal was endorsed by 480 votes to 349.
- On 29 November there followed a meeting of the Northern Ireland Assembly at which Mallon was reinstated as Deputy First Minister and ten other Ministers were appointed in accordance with the agreed procedure.
- Next day the House of Commons and the House of Lords both approved a Devolution Order allowing for the transfer of a range of powers to the Assembly at Stormont. Devolution took effect from midnight on 1 December 1999.
- On 2 December there was a veritable rush of consequential activity. The first meetings took place of the North–South and British–Irish Ministerial Councils; Articles 2 and 3 of Bunreacht na hÉireann were replaced by the new 'aspirational' ones endorsed by the voters of the Republic in the 1998 referendum; and the Executive met for the first time – in the absence of the two DUP ministers.

The DUP's position was interesting. On the one hand, it had not participated in the negotiations that produced the Good Friday Agreement and was totally opposed to virtually every one of its provisions. On the other, it was entitled to two Executive positions on the basis of the number of DUP seats in the Assembly and it was not prepared to allow these to go to other parties by default. So it decided to accept the ministerial jobs, but not to participate in the deliberations of the Executive so long as Sinn Féin was in its membership.

Since it was later to become a matter of contention, we ought also to record here a warning note sounded by the UUP. In agreeing to enter the Executive, the Party said it would be necessary to review progress on decommissioning in February 2000 and if the IRA had not begun the process by then Trimble would resign as First Minister.

'No guns, no government'

Between October and February there was no verifiable or detectable movement by the IRA (or the other paramilitary organisations) on decommissioning, apart from the IRA's initial contact with the de Chastelain Commission. It thus looked as though Trimble's resignation letter – already written and held by a senior UUP colleague – would soon be on its way to the Secretary of State. However, on 10 February Mandelson made a pre-emptive strike and signed an order suspending the operation of the new institutions and reintroducing direct rule. There was thus no need for Trimble to resign, something that many other people in addition to the British government would have regarded as a disaster.

Since the next five months seemed very like a repeat of what had happened in the run-up to the first setting-up of the Executive, we need not go into much detail. The Secretary of State, the Irish Foreign Minister, the Prime Minister and the Taoiseach devoted an inordinate amount of time trying stitch together a deal permitting reinstatement of the Executive. The apparent breakthrough in early May was a proposition from the IRA that it would allow independent international figures to inspect its arms dumps and verify that the weapons remained untouched. As before, there was a carefully orchestrated sequence of events leading up to the publication of the IRA offer:

- On the evening of Friday 7 May the two governments made a joint statement indicating confidence that there were clear proposals for implementing all other aspects of the Agreement and that it was now down to the paramilitary organisations to agree, firmly and finally, that they would put their arms completely and verifiably beyond use. In exchange, the British government would introduce further 'normalisation measures'.
- On Saturday morning, the government wrote jointly to all the political parties setting out its intentions as regards equality, security, policing and prisoners – all of which meshed with the IRA's agenda.
- At lunchtime on Saturday the IRA issued a long statement of its own:
    (i)   it claimed that the leadership of the IRA was committed to a just and lasting peace, as well as to dealing with the arms question;
    (ii) it reiterated the traditional republican doctrine on partition;
    (iii) it confirmed that, in the context of the British government fulfilling its promises on social justice and 'demilitarisation' – code for removing troops and dismantling their installations – the IRA leadership would initiate a process 'that would completely and verifiably put IRA arms beyond use';
    (iv) it stated that the IRA would resume contact with the de Chastelain Commission;
    (v)   most significant of all, it said that 'The contents of a number of our arms dumps will be inspected by agreed third parties who will report that they have done so to the Independent International Commission on Decommissioning. The dumps will be re-inspected regularly to ensure that the weapons have remained silent.'

The UUP's reaction was mixed. A leading member of the 'no' camp, Donaldson, said that there was no sign whatever that the IRA would actually disarm. Trimble, on the other hand, said that the Party would be embarking on a consultation and clarification exercise, but that people were 'encouraged' by the IRA's 'promising statement', which 'appears to break new ground'.

The governments positively welcomed the statement and the Taoiseach was effusive; he said a means had been found to resolve the issue of arms 'once and for all', since the IRA had given an explicit commitment to put arms beyond use 'that could not be clearer'.

A day or so later it was announced that Martti Ahtisaari, a former President of Finland, and Cyril Ramaphosa, former Secretary-General of the African National Congress, had agreed to conduct the inspections of IRA arms dumps. More importantly, Trimble won the argument within the UUP about proceeding to form an Executive; but it was a close call. At a meeting of the Ulster Unionist Council on 27 May his proposal got through by the small margin of 53 per cent to 47 per cent. As a result the Executive resumed its devolved responsibilities at midnight on 30 May.

The main events over the next eight months or so included the following:

- The DUP equivocated about retaking its two ministerial posts but eventually decided to do so – on the basis that there would be a frequent rotation of office holders; by early 2001 this had happened just once. Quite what this was intended to achieve was not fully explained.
- There was a first visit, and an eventual revisit, to an IRA arms dump in the Republic by the international inspectors, who pronounced themselves satisfied on both occasions that the arms were 'beyond use'.
- A bitter feud blew up between the UDA and the UVF, which led to several deaths and to the loyalist areas in which they took place being held in a grip of fear. Against this background, it emerged that the UDA had decided to leave the pro-Agreement camp. Its political counterpart, the UDP, denied that this obliged it too to abandon its support of the Good Friday Agreement.
- The loyalist feud was succeeded by what appeared as a concerted series of pipe-bomb attacks on Catholic homes across Northern Ireland.
- The Saville Tribunal, set up by the British government to revisit the Bloody Sunday deaths, began its hearings in Londonderry's Guildhall. Since most of the information being given to the Tribunal was already in the public domain, a lot of interest focused on the new evidence that there were a few republican gunmen operating in the city on the day in question.
- The UUP leader came under pressure again late in the year from the party grass roots, on the grounds that the IRA had failed to fulfil its undertakings on decommissioning. (Beyond the second visit by Ahtisaari and Ramaphosa, there appeared to have been no further engagement by the IRA either with them or with the de Chastelain Commission.)
- Trimble's margin was even narrower than previously when, at a further meeting of the Ulster Unionist Council, he avoided defeat by announcing that he was withdrawing the 'licence' of the two Sinn Féin ministers to attend meetings of the North–South Council and of the cross-border implementation bodies.

This last had the unavoidable consequence of reopening negotiations about decommissioning, into which were subsumed two other burning issues: first, the SDLP/Sinn Féin claim that reforms to the policing system proposed by the British government did not match up to the Patten recommendations; and, second, Sinn Féin's insistence that the British government had not fulfilled its commitments on demilitarisation – in particular as regards the dismantling of remaining army watchtowers close to the border. In the middle of all this, the RUC announced that recruitment for the new Police Service of Northern Ireland would have to proceed whether there was political agreement or not. Denounced as an attempt to pressurise the SDLP into endorsing prematurely the proposed new policing arrangements, the Chief Constable insisted that the move was necessary to ensure that there would be sufficient trained officers to meet the needs of the community in the foreseeable future.

Once more the Prime Minister and the Taoiseach became involved in trying to broker a compromise, but after more than two months of discussions, completed inconclusively in early March 2001, the 'will they – won't they?' game was obviously still in full swing. In the background, a combination of the CIRA and the RIRA was demonstrating that dissident republicans had not abandoned the armed struggle after all. A particularly sinister turn in the new pattern of violence was a bomb blast outside the BBC's Television Centre in London, not long after a television documentary had named some of those widely thought to have been behind the Omagh bombing.

Yet it is difficult to believe that some kind of overall resolution will not be found, especially given the wider consensus that the new institutions of government in Northern Ireland are working well. However, local government elections and a Westminster general election were looming in June, and the suggestion was that it might suit some parties to defer coming to a conclusion on the three issues at stake – decommissioning, policing and demilitarisation – before they faced the electorate. The worst-case scenario, therefore, was that the Executive would be suspended once again and a new accommodation hammered out later in the year.

Can the new system of government work?

Let us assume that it will be possible to overcome the present difficulties and that a wider social stability can be also established in Northern Ireland. The new structures of government are certainly novel; the main question is, then, can they endure? The present writers have discussed elsewhere whether the new institutions arising out of the Good Friday Agreement meet a number of criteria for success; we concluded that 'the most important elements for stable democracy in Northern Ireland are now present'.[13] That said, there do seem to be some potential difficulties, relating in particular to the practical operation of the system. A few examples will suffice.

First, parties that achieve a relatively small proportion of the popular vote are guaranteed a ministerial post or posts in government. This has implications for the future development of party structures. For example, in policy terms there is now little to choose between the SDLP and Sinn Féin, but with assured places in government there is no immediate incentive for either of them to want to 'tidy up' the party map. This also means that the political competition 'internal' to each section of the community will continue, requiring parties to do battle almost entirely on the basis of which one of them can be shown to be most vigorous in defence of its 'own' people's interests. What is likely to be sacrificed, then, is a hoped for reconciliation – even just a *modus vivendi* – between the two communities and the elimination of sectarian tensions in the longer term.

Given the inevitably conflicting views of Northern Ireland's future held by Executive members, another problematic area lies somewhere between the traditional liberal democratic concepts of ministerial responsibility and Cabinet responsibility. For there will plainly be much more strain – and indeed temptation to break ranks – on 'responsibility' questions than in a traditional one-party or agreed coalition government. It is hardly surprising that decisions and actions taken by ministers are being closely scrutinised by people seeking evidence of bias towards their 'own side'. What is not reassuring is that some ministers have themselves displayed a disposition to do this in respect of Executive colleagues from opposing parties.

Other difficulties might arise from the sheer unwieldiness of the policy-making process. Thus, in regard to some relatively innocuous matter of public policy, it is not just civil servants, a minister, the Executive and the Assembly that will apply their attention to it:

• the Assembly committee 'shadowing' a minister has a 'policy development, scrutinising and advisory role' to which heed must be paid;
• involved also may be the equivalent minister in the Republic, wearing a North–South Council hat and seeking coordination of policy across the two jurisdictions;
• in such a case there will nearly always be a cross-border implementation body, with which consultation will be essential;
• finally, there may also be UK-wide and EU implications, demanding the drawing in of still more extraneous sources of policy advice and policy formation.

Another point of difficulty arises from the fact that the Minister of Finance has negligible tax-raising powers. This means, as we have already noted, that this minister's role is primarily as a lobbyist to the Treasury in London, seeking as much money as possible for expenditure by Northern Ireland departments. This was precisely the situation under the system of government that existed until 1972; and what it meant was that there was little scope for initiative and imagination on the part of ministers in Belfast. There were some important and interesting exceptions, but for most purposes Stormont was a rubber-stamp Parliament. It is hard to accept that a lively and industrious Assembly and Executive, out to show the voters that the new institutions can make a real difference to the way Northern Ireland is governed, will not be seeking more control over fiscal decision-making in the near future – from a Treasury that will be very reluctant to grant it.

Conclusion

Despite such reservations, we need to recognise that historic compromises have been made, innovative political structures designed and new partnerships forged. Put simply, a huge amount of change has been accomplished in Northern Ireland in a relatively short time. We have touched on almost all of this in the course of this chapter, but two changes in particular deserve to be drawn out. First, notwithstanding the elimination of the 1985 Anglo-Irish Agreement, the Irish Republic appears to retain a virtually unchallenged right to an input into the way a part of the UK is governed and administered. Though perhaps an outrage to those devoted to the immutable sovereignty of the British Parliament, this constitutional novelty has raised barely a ripple of complaint from the great majority of the members of that Parliament. Moreover, it is clear that it would be of value to grow the same kind of arrangements in other conflict situations where there are harmful social and political divisions resting on ethnicity, religion or national allegiance.

Second – and arguably the other side of that sovereignty coin – all substantial components of the Irish nationalist tradition have endorsed the right of unionists, for so long as they remain a majority, to keep Northern Ireland a part of the UK – and thus perpetuate in formal legal terms the partition of Ireland. This is important not just because it represents the settled 'self-determination' of the whole of the Irish people in the referendums of 1998: it is significant also because it involves an at least implicit acknowledgement that unionists are the real 'British presence' in Northern Ireland.

Notes

1 For administrative and local government reasons Ireland had come to be divided into thirty-two counties. Those included in Northern Ireland were, in alphabetical order, Antrim, Armagh, Down, Fermanagh, Londonderry (which people of a nationalist disposition call Derry – the 'London' having been added to mark British colonisation) and Tyrone. Some republicans/nationalists also describe Northern Ireland as 'the Six Counties' and the rest of Ireland as 'the Twenty-Six Counties'.

2 Despite the exclusion of the counties of Cavan, Donegal and Monaghan, most unionists continue to describe Northern Ireland as Ulster; and 'Ulster' forms part of the title of most unionist political and paramilitary organisations – on which see more below.

3 For evidence of early official concern, see *Disturbances in Northern Ireland: Report of the Commission Appointed by the Governor of Northern Ireland*, Belfast: HMSO, 1969 (the Cameron Report). R. Cormack and R. Osborne (eds), *Religion, Education and Employment: Aspects of Equal Opportunity in Northern Ireland*, Belfast: Appletree, 1983, remains a valuable overview.

4 The definitive story of the Northern Ireland civil rights movement can be found in B. Purdie, *Politics on the Streets*, Belfast: Blackstaff, 1990.

5 P. Arthur and K. Jeffrey, *Northern Ireland Since 1968*, 2nd edition, Oxford: Blackwell, 1996, p. 56.

6 Quoted in P. Buckland, *The Factory of Grievances: Devolved Government in Northern Ireland 1922–1939*, Dublin: Gill & Macmillan, 1979, p. 72.

7 See, for example, T. Cradden, *Trade Unionism, Socialism & Partition: The Labour Movement in Northern Ireland 1939–1953*, Belfast: December Books, 1993.

8 In keeping with long-standing Sinn Féin policy, both men refused to take their seats in the British Parliament.

9 D. Fell, 'Building a better economy', *TSB Economic and Business Review*, Vol. 1, No. 3, 1986, pp. 22–5.

10 See J. Considine and E. O'Leary, 'The growth performance of Northern Ireland and the Republic of Ireland: 1960 to 1995', in N. Collins (ed.), *Political Issues in Ireland Today*, Manchester: Manchester University Press, 2nd edition, 1999.

11 The account of events between the summer of 1996 and early 2001 which follows relies on T. Cradden and N. Collins, 'The Northern Ireland Peace Agreement', in N. Collins (ed.), *Political Issues in Ireland Today*, Manchester: Manchester University Press, 2nd edition, 1999, and the University of Ulster CAIN website – at http://cain.ulst.ac.uk.

12 For an accessible full text of the Good Friday Agreement, see the *Irish Times* website – at http://www.Ireland.com.

13 Cradden and Collins, 'The Northern Ireland Peace Agreement', pp. 204–5.

Further reading

Arthur, P., *Special Relationships: Britain, Ireland and the Northern Ireland Problem*, London: Routledge, 2001.

Bardon, J., *A History of Ulster*, Belfast: Blackstaff, 1992.

Bew, P. and Gillespie, G., *Northern Ireland: A Chronology of the Troubles 1968–1999*, Dublin: Gill & Macmillan, 1999.

Connolly, M., *Politics and Policy-Making in Northern Ireland*, Hemel Hempstead: Philip Allen, 1990.

Cox, M., Guelke, A. and Stephen, F. (eds), *A Farewell to Arms? From 'Long War' to Long Peace in Northern Ireland*, Manchester: Manchester University Press, 2000.

Elliott, S. and Flakes, W. D., *Northern Ireland: A Political Directory 1968–1999*, Belfast: Blackstaff, 1999.

McKittrick, D. and McVea, D., *Making Sense of the Troubles*, Belfast: Blackstaff, 2000.

Whyte, J., *Interpreting Northern Ireland*, Oxford: Oxford University Press, 1990.

Wright, F., *Northern Ireland: A Comparative Analysis*, 2nd edition, Dublin: Gill & Macmillan, 1992.

8

External relations

Ireland's place in the world economic order (as discussed in Chapter 1) influences its relations with other countries to a very great degree. Countries with which Ireland has significant trading relations are obviously the object of much government and private attention. Indeed, the establishment of Ireland's embassies, consulates and missions is guided in large part by considerations of trade. But other factors are also important: the pattern of Irish migration in this and previous generations; the spread of Irish missionary efforts; and the desire to forge a distinctive Irish foreign policy. In this chapter, the range of Ireland's relations with other countries is outlined, giving special attention to Britain, the United States, the EU and the United Nations.

A feature of Irish foreign policy that marks it off from that of Britain and the United States is its neutrality. Both these countries are part of the North Atlantic Treaty Organisation (NATO), an alliance formed after the Second World War to resist the threat of Soviet expansion. Most members of NATO had been parties to the war and so too had most of its counterparts in the Warsaw Pact – the Soviet bloc's equivalent of NATO. Ireland, however, remained neutral and has maintained this stance ever since. Although neutrality had been a recurring theme in nationalist thinking for some time, the initial decision was almost entirely driven by the state of Anglo-Irish relations: the Irish government saw involvement in an alliance which included the UK as incompatible with the claim that Northern Ireland was part of the national territory. While the original decision was an essentially pragmatic one, however, neutrality has come to be seen by many people as an enduring assertion of the independence of the Irish state. There have, on the other hand, been calls in some quarters recently for a review of the policy, especially since the EU's Maastricht Treaty established the concept of a Common Foreign and Security Policy (CFSP) (on which see more below).

Relations with Britain

Ireland's relations with Britain are fashioned by a range of inter-related factors. The relationship is complex, involved and multifaceted: the Republic is the only country with which the UK has a land border; many thousands of Irish citizens live in Britain (but have never been considered foreigners); for many professional, cultural, sporting and other social purposes, the two islands are treated jointly; British companies have invested readily in Ireland; Britain takes approximately one-quarter of Irish exports; Ireland is Britain's seventh largest export market; and even though Ireland became a republic in 1948, it has retained the favoured status usually enjoyed only by countries of the British Commonwealth. And yet, as we have seen, Northern Ireland is an important issue in both countries; it sometimes intrudes a jarring note into the development of policy, economic activity and social exchange that would otherwise have been expected to progress harmoniously.

The relations between Ireland and Britain are conditioned by a number of asymmetries of power. Britain is a large, highly developed state, which, while no longer the great and utterly self-confident power it once was, participates much more centrally than Ireland in world affairs. The British political leadership continues to see its international role as a significant one – in relation to world trade, military matters (including nuclear deterrence), scientific research and cultural endeavour. British diplomats, military personnel and business people are actively engaged in almost every major theatre of world affairs, through treaty obligations, vestiges of colonial responsibilities and economic self-interest.

Many small countries with powerful neighbours find it difficult to come to terms with their relatively minor place in the larger world's view. In Ireland's case, this difficulty is intensified by its former place in the British Empire. Some observers have argued that many components of Irish foreign policy arise purely from the need to assert the nation's status as an independent actor on a wider stage. As a consequence, Ireland pursues an active foreign policy on issues of no immediate material advantage to itself; often, though not by contrivance, it takes a contrary view to the UK on such issues.

For Ireland, nationalism is the dominant ideology. It binds diverse individuals into 'a people', acts as a motive for economic, cultural and sporting achievement, and provides a source of genuine pride and sympathy. The nation has become the highest affiliation and obligation of the individual, and through it a significant part of personal identity is formed. For some Irish people, however, much of the definition of that identity is found in contradistinction to a British identity. National achievement is frequently measured relative to Britain, and to do better than England in particular is sufficient to define success. This attitude is inevitably reflected in matters of public policy. Issues are defined in nationalist terms very readily, and injustices, insults, ingratitude or ungraciousness to any one Irish person by 'the British' (in whatever form) is regarded as an injury to all. British politicians and bureaucrats are often insensitive to Irish nationalism; while they may treat other groups equally cavalierly, in Ireland such treatment is often seen as evidence of British antagonism, disrespect or disinterest.

Relations between Britain and Ireland are further complicated by the degree of attention each pays to the other. In Britain, domestic Irish politics (or at least that portion not relating directly to Northern Ireland) get similar coverage in the media to that given to the politics of France or Germany – sometimes less. By contrast, not only does the Irish media devote considerable space to British affairs, but British television and newspapers are freely and widely available. The reverse is not true. The Irish public is thus more aware of, and informed about, events in Britain than about events in any other country with which Ireland has dealings. The ready movement of Irish people to and from Britain, for business and social reasons, reinforces this high level of British media penetration. Moreover, the easy communications between Ireland and Britain help solidify the generally favourable image of British people in Ireland.

These friendly attitudes do not extend, however, to the British government and 'Establishment'. Images of British institutions, as opposed to individuals, are mediated by the predominant nationalistic historical interpretation of the role of the British in denying Ireland independence for so long. As a result, Irish public policy with respect to Britain has, until recently, been officially cautious, occasionally suspicious and always watchful. Since the Anglo-Irish Agreement in 1985, however, senior politicians and public officials enjoy useful, regular and friendly relations with their British counterparts. The two governments now work closely on Northern Ireland policy and this cooperation has had an impact in other areas. It remains to be said that policy ideas, public inquiries, official reports and legislation originating in Britain remain among the most pervasive outside influences on Irish politics today.

Relations with the United States

Remarkably, Irish political relations with America also have much to do with Anglo-Irish relations. The United States, with its substantial ethnic Irish community, has often been considered as a potentially powerful ally in arguments with Britain over Northern Ireland. Such an outlook is ironic in that British politicians have since 1945 laid great stress on their 'special relationship' with America.

The attitudes of Irish-Americans, particularly those who identify emotionally with Ireland, are heavily tutored by their forebears' experience. This was of rural Ireland under British political and landlord rule, and of America as a hopeful new home for poor emigrants. For Irish-Americans who have not prospered, Britain remains a *bête noire*; and even among those who have

enjoyed social and economic success in America, old images remain important. Yet many Irish-Americans do not have any sustained, personal and direct
experience of Ireland, and their ethnic sentiment, money and influence have
often been used in ways that Irish governments find unhelpful – to say the
least. As a result, much of Ireland's considerable diplomatic effort in America
has been directed towards 're-educating' Irish-American opinion, which has
often been more intensely anti-British than domestic opinion.

Relations with the United States have been markedly assisted in recent
years by the active involvement of the 'Friends of Ireland', a group of Democratic and Republican Representatives and Senators strongly influenced by
contacts with John Hume of the SDLP. The Friends have worked closely with
Irish diplomats to help in the dissemination of the Irish government's case for
peaceful reform in Northern Ireland. However, other Irish-American groups –
such as Noraid (formerly a registered IRA fund-raising body in the United
States), the Irish National Caucus (which sought to publicise the wrongs
suffered by Catholics in Northern Ireland) and the Ad Hoc Congressional
Committee on Irish Affairs – together pressed forward a more republican
interpretation of events in Northern Ireland.

Irish political influence on American policy has traditionally been greater
in the legislature than in the executive branch, however, although there are
some barriers to Irish influence. Britain's sway in the State Department (the
American department of foreign affairs) and the Department of Defense has
always been sufficient to counter any unwelcome Irish manoeuvre. Irish
neutrality during the Second World War, as unpopular in the United States as
it was in the UK, has faded as a contentious issue; but Britain's centrality to
American intelligence gathering and other military involvement continues to
be crucial. Further, the extensive economic and financial links between the
United States and Britain are a significant factor in ensuring that the two
countries' relations remain politically harmonious.

For all that, as we have seen on Chapter 7, under the 1992–2000 Clinton
administration, the politics of the Northern Ireland question received much
greater presidential attention than ever before. Clinton showed a close personal interest in the problem and members of his personal staff were actively
involved in promoting peace initiatives of various kinds. The President took a
particular risk (by some accounts against State Department advice) in permitting the leader of Sinn Féin, Gerry Adams, to make a high-profile trip to
America in 1994, soon after the IRA and UVF/UDA cease-fires had been
called. Moreover, Clinton demonstrated his own personal commitment to the
quest for peace by visiting Ireland three times during his term of office. Irish–
American relations are close, therefore, and usually become contentious only
when British interests are at issue. They will surely continue to be close while
Ireland remains such an attractive location for American investment.

In addition to that, some 40 million Americans claim Irish origin; and
while large-scale emigration from Ireland to the United States effectively

ended in the mid-1960s, many young Irish people continue to seek employment there. Ireland thus retains important resources of goodwill, sentimental attachment and mutual economic self-interest in the United States.

The relationship with the EU

Many nationalist-minded people heralded Ireland's entry in 1973 to what is now called the EU as a chance to lessen decisively the influence of Britain on Irish life. It has indeed had a major impact and Irish enthusiasm for Europe remains high. For a small state with a relatively open economy, participation in the EU has meant great economic opportunities and unusual political influence. When Ireland holds the presidency of Europe (as it does on a rotational basis), Irish ministers play a more significant role on the world stage. At the same time, leaders of the Irish business community and senior public servants have seen the EU as an opportunity to develop their talents in a wider setting. There has of course been some resistance to the EU, from groups who are concerned about the loss of Irish sovereignty but, overall, Ireland sees itself as an approving, active, enthusiastic and cooperative member.

Not least among the reasons for this is that, since accession, Ireland has received considerable financial transfers from EU funds. Arguably the major recent development within the EU was the creation in 1992 of the 'Single Market', which, virtually at a stroke, eliminated almost all the barriers to trade between member states. Trade with other EU states has been a critical factor in Ireland's impressive economic growth and healthy surplus in the balance of payments. In preparation for 1992, the EU provided considerable assistance to the poorer parts of the Union, which brought the net transfers to Ireland from its accession to around IR£20 billion. Europe also provided earmarked funding for economic development in border areas, from which both parts of Ireland benefited. Indeed, as late as the mid-1990s, approximately 8 per cent of the government's current budget came from Brussels – funding which Irish officials were vigorous and assiduous in gaining. However, the period during which Ireland has been in receipt of significant EU subvention is rapidly coming to a close. Because of its remarkable economic performance, as well as the expansion of the EU to the east, Ireland no longer figures in any of the EU's major categories justifying special financial support. Indeed, Ireland will soon, for the first time, become a net contributor to the EU's coffers.

Ireland's interests in Brussels are, like those of all member states, looked after by the country's Permanent Representation. This is a body akin to an embassy, which services important EU committees, the main one being the Committee of Permanent Representatives of member states. In addition, Irish ministers and officials attend numerous EU meetings, ranging from the weekly management meeting to regulate certain farm commodities to those of the European Council itself. As was seen in Chapter 4, EU directives and regulations have considerable impact on domestic policies, often in areas where Irish thinking was previously underdeveloped.

The EU has developed politically since the original Treaty of Rome. The Treaty on European Union – the 'Maastricht Treaty' – came into force in November 1993. It provided for further economic and monetary union between EU states and called for the development of the CFSP. The Treaty was endorsed in Ireland by a referendum. It nevertheless represents a significant political challenge – all the more so since the EU is likely to enlarge in the next decade to include several further nations in eastern and southern Europe. The impetus for enlargement comes from the security and economic interests of several current member states, most notably Germany.

For Ireland, as already noted, enlargement may be costly in the longer term, because the institutional arrangements and financial benefits of the EU will have to change to take account of the new members and their needs. In institutional terms, furthermore, smaller states such as Ireland will have to accept a decline in their political independence as a price for greater European integration. National governments will have to accept more majority voting (as opposed to the unanimity which has often been required up to now for changes in European law and regulations), presenting the possibility of having to abide by decisions with which they strongly disagree. Also, more power will probably be given to the European Parliament, in which the Republic has only fifteen of the 626 seats. The right of smaller states to nominate a member of the European Commission has already come under scrutiny, and it seems likely that the situation at present, whereby Ireland is entitled to a permanent member, will have to come to an end.

The ambition to create a CFSP developed out of the experience of, first, European Political Cooperation (EPC) and, second, the Western European Union. For twenty-two years under EPC, all EU member states sought to coordinate their foreign policy. EPC was not particularly constraining on member states, but it did allow some mutual cooperation on a number of occasions: during the upheavals in Afghanistan; concerning NATO's deployment of nuclear weapons; through the period of the collapse of the Soviet Union; and following the reunification of Germany. CFSP extends the EPC approach but, crucially for Ireland, looks towards a common defence policy.

Important questions have already arisen for Ireland out of the rethinking that is taking place, especially in regard to the European 'Partnership for Peace' and the European Rapid Reaction Force. The Fianna Fáil/PD government has already made controversial commitments in principle to both these EU-inspired initiatives, even though they appear to represent a moving on from the notion of the Common European Foreign and *Security* Policy towards a common *defence* policy – something that might well call Ireland's traditional neutrality into question. Needless to say, there has begun to be debate in Ireland on this question. Opponents of neutrality say that Ireland should not attempt to hold back the development of a common EU defence policy. Playing a part in defending Europe against attack is, it is argued, a moral obligation on all those countries which would benefit from any agreed defence arrangements. Those who favour maintaining neutrality point to the advantages to Europe, and even to the rest of the world, of having at least one neutral member of the EU.

The most pressing decision for Ireland in its relations with the EU in the mid-1990s was whether to become part of the Economic and Monetary Union (EMU) scheduled to be fully in place by January 2002. EMU involves a common currency, the euro, which is controlled by the ECB in Frankfurt. To prepare for this development, member states had to achieve certain monetary targets and Ireland met these without difficulty. It became clear at an early stage, however, that the UK, including of course Northern Ireland, would not be joining – certainly not immediately. The dilemma for Ireland was thus whether to proceed in the absence of what was still its major trading partner. There was first of all the prospect of a difficult to manage EMU/non-EMU border in Ireland; but the real danger was felt to be that a devalued sterling would make Irish goods uncompetitive in Britain. On the other hand, EMU membership seemed likely to bring important political and economic benefits. Ireland would enjoy lower interest rates, inflation and transaction (money exchange) costs. It would also give all the EMU countries a general economic boost.

In the event, the decision was made to join the EMU. To the surprise of many it was the euro that fell steeply in value, giving Ireland the currency advantage in its trading relations with the UK, rather than the other way about. However, there is no doubt that the EMU has made the internal management of the economy in Ireland more problematical, since decisions of the ECB are plainly influenced more by the major players like France and Germany than by a small country like Ireland. For example, the Governor of the Central Bank of Ireland has made no secret of the fact that, left to its own devices, Ireland would have had a very different interest rate regime in place than that imposed from Frankfurt in 1999/2000. The Governor remains nonetheless a supporter of EMU and, like many other people in positions of influence, he feels it to be crucial that Ireland has remained a part of the 'inner circle' of European states.

Relations with the United Nations

Ireland's activist and enthusiastic stance in relation to international organisations like the United Nations (UN) began in the 1920s and 1930s. The Free State's membership of the League of Nations was an important assertion of nationhood. De Valera, in particular, ensured that Ireland's pacific voice was heard in the 1930s, when Italian and German military policies were disturbing the world order. Until the mid-1950s, Ireland was excluded from the League's effective successor, the UN, because of a Soviet veto. However, it was again a de Valera government that brought Ireland back into membership, in 1957 – signalling an activist stance on contentious issues such as China's representation at the UN, arms control and disarmament.

In both the League and the UN, Ireland has been a constant advocate of giving maximum authority to the world body in settling disputes. Despite neutrality, for example, Ireland allowed US planes bound for the 1990 war with Iraq to refuel at Shannon Airport, because the American action had UN authority. Ireland is also strongly committed to UN peacekeeping and has sent troops to the Congo, Cyprus, Lebanon, Sinai and the Iran/Iraq border. A source of much national satisfaction is that between 1958 and the mid-1990s, more than 42,000 Irish soldiers served with the UN in peacekeeping and other humanitarian tasks. Even greater satisfaction was occasioned in 2000 when Ireland gained a seat on the UN Security Council. Regarded as a diplomatic triumph for such a small nation, it was also seen as an important recognition of Ireland's firm commitment to the UN down the years.

Other external commitments

As we noted in Chapter 2, Ireland has another important European commitment, outside the EU. The 1950 European Convention on Human Rights is one of the most important of a large number of international declarations of rights made since 1945. In contrast with the UN's 1948 Universal Declaration of Human Rights and the subsequent UN charters of rights, the European Convention has an important element of collective enforcement (see also Chapter 5).

Since the late 1950s, Ireland has been a member of several other major international organisations: the International Monetary Fund; the International Bank for Reconstruction and Development; the International Finance Corporation; and the International Development Association. Ireland is a founder member of the Organisation for Economic Cooperation and Development, which, together with its affiliates, helps the twenty-nine member countries' governments with the formulation of economic and social policy. Its reports are often a focus of debate in Ireland, because of their wide comparative analysis and authoritative style.

In common with other countries, Ireland uses its assistance to developing countries as part of its foreign policy. Ireland spent well over IR£106 million in 2000 (0.3 per cent of GNP) on development assistance to Third World countries. This represents more than a doubling since 1992, although there are frequent complaints that the amount still falls seriously short of the UN target of 0.7 per cent of GNP. Approximately 40 per cent of total aid is expended on bilateral assistance (direct Irish aid to developing countries) and the rest is given to international organisations to support their development activities. Over 60 per cent of bilateral aid is spent on projects in Ireland's six priority sub-Saharan countries: Ethiopia, Uganda, Lesotho, Tanzania, Zambia and the Sudan. The largest sectors for expenditure are agricultural and rural development, education and training. The aim of the aid is to reduce poverty, foster democracy, respond to disasters and contribute to building civil society and social solidarity. It is possible that Mozambique will be added to the list of priority countries, as Ireland's aid budget increases.

Conclusion

As in many other countries, external relations are often discussed in Ireland in terms of sovereignty. The idea that a nation state should have power and control over its own future is very strongly held. In reality, Ireland is as constrained in foreign affairs as it is in other areas of policy by its position in the world economy. Additionally, it is influenced by the same tight network of international obligations, organisations and agreements as most other countries today. Indeed, while the Republic of Ireland now has all the symbols of independence, the level of its interdependence with the rest of the world has never been greater. Nation states no longer have complete and actual control over the direction of policy in their own territory, even if they do so formally. There are clearly difficulties, therefore, in analysing external relations in terms of purely formal sovereignty.

To begin with, the world economic system serves to limit the autonomy of national governments. In Chapter 1, we examined Ireland's place in the international division of labour and saw that it competed with other small countries for international investment. Multinational companies, for which national boundaries are less important than comparative costs and opportunities, play a key role in this global system. For such companies, technological advances in communications and transportation have eroded the relevance of independent national economic policies. Ireland's foreign policy is thus aimed in part at protecting the Irish economy from the vagaries of the world economic order – by cooperating with other countries for the coordination of policy. To a degree, therefore, sovereignty is now about collective action by states.

The demands of mutual defence erode sovereignty also. Irish foreign policy will soon have to come to terms with greater European cooperation on defence, with the obvious difficulties which this presents for neutrality. The pressure for a European defence policy is itself a product of the changes within the hegemonic power blocs that dominate world politics. Most of Ireland's EU partners are part of an alliance which limits them as autonomous military actors. NATO nations do retain the capacity for independent military action, but they also recognise the reality of collective security. Although not all

NATO countries participate fully, the existence of an integrated supranational command structure ensures that, in certain military crises, 'national armies' will operate under supreme allied command. Given that its partners have qualified their national sovereignty in the name of collective defence, it is likely that this is the model which will be used to shape any specifically EU security arrangements. More important, however, are the doubts about the continuation of an American commitment to the defence of Europe (especially since the beginning in 2001 of the Bush presidency) and about the effects of political ferment in the former communist countries in Eastern Europe. These will present Western Europe with new political and military choices, for which Ireland may have to assume some responsibility.

The rapidly changing context in which Ireland arranges its external relations involves the world economic order, international treaties, other countries' arrangements for collective defence, international law and the EU. All of these may appear to undermine Ireland's independence of action – its sovereignty. In fact, many of the obligations and constraints which arise from all this represent an enhancement of Ireland's potential as an economic and political actor. The EU, in particular, protects the national economy, the environment and human potential of its citizens. It certainly allows Ireland to make a more significant impact on world developments – on world politics today – than it otherwise could.

Further reading

Arthur, P., *Special Relationships: Britain, Ireland and the Northern Ireland Problem*, London: Routledge, 2001.

Holmes, M., Rees, N. and Whelan, B., *The Poor Relation: Irish Foreign Policy and The Third World*, Dublin: Gill & Macmillan, 1993.

Keatinge, P., *A Singular Stance: Irish Neutrality in the 1980s*, Dublin: Institute of Public Administration, 1984.

Keatinge, P. (ed.), *Ireland and EC Membership Evaluated*, London: Frances Pinter, 1991.

Scott, D., *Ireland and the IGC*, Dublin: Institute for European Affairs, 1996.

Index

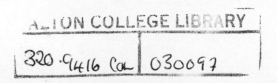